Scale To Last

A Practical Playbook to Design, Form,
Launch, Scale, and Successfully Exit Your
Organization With Lasting Legacy

Dr. Assegid (AZ) Habtewold

*The ultimate guide to starting with clarity, building on
strong foundations, scaling with strategy and confidence,
and exiting successfully so you can create a thriving
organization, build lasting value, and leave a legacy that
endures.*

ISBN– 13: 978-1-947524-24-8
ISBN– 10: 1-947524-24-0

Printed in the United States of America

Published February 2026

AZ

The A to Z Publications

Table of Contents

INTRODUCTION

What It Takes to Build Something That Lasts

"Organizations are not built in a day. They are built every day, through the small decisions that accumulate into a legacy." **Peter Drucker***,* Organizational Development and Management Consultant

For years, For years, I believed I had built a company. I had clients, impact, credibility, and what I thought was flexibility. Then I spent an extended period overseas, living between two worlds across the Atlantic. What was meant to be restorative became clarifying. My expenses doubled. My responsibilities followed me. But my income stayed exactly where it was. Not because demand disappeared or the market shifted — but because nothing worked without me.

If I didn't show up, decisions stalled. If I didn't work, revenue slowed. If I stopped, everything stopped. That was the moment I faced a hard truth: <u>I wasn't running a business. I was running myself.</u> What I had built was meaningful and stable — but fragile. It could survive effort, not absence. It could sustain work, not distance. And it could not outlast me.

That realization changed how I understood scale. Scale is not about getting bigger. It is about becoming independent of any one person — including the founder. And legacy is not created by staying forever. It is created by building something strong enough to last even when you don't. That is what this book is about.

Why Organizations Exist

At some point, every serious builder confronts a limit. One person can carry a vision. One person can work relentlessly. One person can even spark change. But one person cannot execute a big vision alone — nor sustain it over time. Impact stalls when effort remains personal. Organizations exist to break that constraint.

They are not just legal entities or operating structures. They are mechanisms for scale, continuity, and shared execution. An organization allows impact to move beyond a single mind, a single body, or a single lifetime. Organizations make it possible to:

- Execute visions too large for any one person
- Multiply effort through coordinated teams
- Distribute judgment instead of centralizing decisions
- Sustain impact beyond the founder's presence
- Preserve values, standards, and intent over time
- Leave a legacy that continues after you step away — or pass on

Without an organization, impact remains personal. With one, impact becomes institutional.

The Gap Between Hustle and Structural Reality

Most organizations never scale. They may start, launch, survive, and even succeed — but very few grow beyond their founder. Fewer still create durable influence, transferable value, or clean exit options. Across industries, the pattern repeats. Early traction validates the idea. Demand increases. Complexity follows — and strain appears. Decisions bottleneck. Processes break. Culture becomes inconsistent. Growth feels heavier instead of freeing. Founders begin asking familiar questions:

- Why does everything still depend on me?
- Why does growth feel chaotic instead of strategic?
- Why are we busy but not profitable?

- Why does scaling feel risky instead of exciting?

These are not signs of failure. They are signals of a structural ceiling — one created long before scaling was attempted.

The Scaling Ceiling No One Warns You About

Scaling amplifies whatever already exists. If clarity exists, scale multiplies it. If confusion exists, scale spreads it. Scale does not fix problems — it exposes them. Organizations stall not because they lack effort or ambition, but because *they were never designed for scale*. Informal decision-making, founder-dependent operations, weak financial discipline, and culture held together by proximity cannot survive growth. Pushing harder rarely works. Redesigning what should have been built earlier does.

Foundation Determines Whether Scale Is Possible

Every organization carries its future inside its early decisions — about purpose, structure, systems, leadership, and exit. These decisions determine whether an organization can move beyond the founder, handle complexity, attract capital, retain talent, scale profitably, and exit successfully. Weak foundations may survive at a small scale. They almost never survive growth. Strong foundations do something different. They make scaling repeatable, leadership distributable, and value transferable. They make *Scale to Last* possible.

What This Book Is — and Is Not

This book is not about chasing size for its own sake. It is about building organizations that can grow without breaking. Organizations that scale successfully: <u>design with scale in mind, even when small, form structures that can carry growth, stabilize before expanding, choose scaling paths intentionally, prepare for exit early, knowing scale without transferability has limits.</u> Scale is not a phase you enter. It is a capability you earn.

What If I Plan to Exit Early?

Some founders do not intend to stabilize or scale the organization themselves. Their goal is to design, form, launch — and exit early by selling the company, bringing in investors, or handing growth to the next operator. This book is for them too.

Early exit does not eliminate the need for scale-ready design. It increases it. Buyers and investors pay premiums for optionality — the ability to scale without rebuilding the foundation. That optionality is created long before scale ever happens. This book does not assume you must be the one to scale the organization. It assumes someone will — and they will pay more if you've designed it well.

Why This Book Exists

This book is for founders who want more than survival — who want to grow beyond themselves, build transferable value, and exit on their terms. It is for those at the beginning, the middle, and the edge of transition — and for leaders and advisors who understand that real scale is designed, not discovered. *Scale to Last* follows the full organizational lifecycle:

1. Purpose & Design
2. Form & Legalize
3. Launch & Stabilize
4. Scale & Exit

Scaling is not about becoming bigger. It is about becoming stronger, more durable, and less dependent on the founder. If you are serious about building something that lasts beyond you, you are in the right place. Now, let's begin.

PART I

PURPOSE & DESIGN

"Design is not just what it looks like and feels like. Design is how it works."
Steve Jobs, Co-Founder of Apple

Clarify purpose. Define value. Design intentionally. Build the blueprint before the building.

E veryone builds something. Building is not the problem. The real question is *why an organization should exist at all.* One person can carry a vision. One person can work relentlessly. One person can even create early impact. But no individual can execute a meaningful vision at scale, sustain it over time, or ensure it survives their absence. Purpose is what justifies forming an organization instead of remaining a solo effort.

Why Purpose Comes Before Design

Organizations exist to solve problems that are larger than any one person and longer than any one career. They are mechanisms for continuity, coordination, and shared execution. <u>When purpose is clear, design has direction. When purpose is vague, design compensates with effort.</u>

Without explicit purpose, organizations drift into activity without alignment. With it, design becomes intentional, scalable, and transferable.

Design Is Not the Problem, Designing Without Purpose Is

Everyone builds something. Building is not the problem. The real challenge is what you build for. Most founders are taught how to start. Very few are taught how to design for scale. As a result, <u>many organizations are built for momentum, not longevity. They are optimized for launch, not growth.</u> They rely on founder energy instead of systems that can carry weight over time. When purpose and design are weak or rushed, organizations fall into predictable traps:

- They solve immediate problems without anticipating complexity
- They build around people instead of processes
- They design for speed, not scalability
- They confuse activity with progress
- They grow demand faster than the structure can support

Design is not cosmetic. It is structural. And ***when design is flawed, scaling does not fix it*** — scaling exposes it.

Design Determines Whether Scale Is Survivable

Many founders believe design happens after success. In reality, design determines whether success is even survivable. Design is the discipline of deciding before you are forced to decide. It requires clarity around: purpose, identity, business model, structure, and strategic vehicle These decisions are often made implicitly, yet they shape everything that follows. When design is intentional:

- Growth becomes manageable, not chaotic
- Leadership becomes distributable, not founder-dependent
- Systems replace derring-do
- Value becomes transferable
- Scaling becomes less risky
- Exit conversations focus on valuation, not survival

When design is accidental, founders become bottlenecks, decisions slow as complexity increases, culture fragments, systems lag behind demand, growth becomes expensive and fragile, and valuation suffers due to risk and dependence. Poorly designed organizations rarely fail loudly at first. They bleed value quietly over time.

Most Scaling Failures Begin as Design Failures

Organizations rarely fail because of one bad decision at scale. They fail because of small design decisions made early — or avoided altogether.

- An unclear problem leads to scattered offerings
- A vague purpose leads to misaligned priorities
- A weak business model leads to growth without profit
- The wrong structure limits capital, talent, and exit options
- The wrong strategic vehicle makes scaling expensive or impossible

These issues may not matter at ten customers. They become fatal at ten thousand.

Design Is About Capacity, Not Control

Many founders resist design because they fear rigidity. But good design does not constrain growth. It creates capacity. Design done well allows an organization to absorb demand without chaos, delegate decisions without confusion, onboard people without cultural drift, attract capital without structural friction, scale without losing its soul. *Design skipped early takes freedom away later.*

What Part I Will Help You Do

Part I focuses on designing with the end in mind — not just the end of launch, but the end of founder dependence, early-stage fragility, operational chaos, stalled growth, and missed exit opportunities. Specifically, this part will help you:

1. Define a problem worth solving at scale

2. Clarify PURPOSE beyond personal passion
3. Design an identity that survives growth
4. Build a business model that sustains expansion
5. Choose a structure that supports capital, talent, and exit
6. Select the right strategic vehicle for your goals

This is not theoretical work. It is pre-engineering for scale.

Design Sets the Ceiling for Scale

There is a limit to how far an organization can grow without redesign. That limit is set early. Design determines:

- How fast you can grow
- How complex you can become
- How independent the organization can be from you
- How attractive it is to investors and acquirers
- How clean your exit can be

If you design for today only, tomorrow will punish you. If you design for scale, tomorrow becomes optional — not overwhelming.

A Note for Founders Who Have Already Started

If you have already formed or launched your organization, this part still applies. Refining purpose and design is not a one-time event. *It must be revisited whenever growth introduces new complexity* — new people, markets, systems, or pressure. The next three chapters are not only about starting well. They are about redesigning intentionally — surfacing implicit decisions, identifying structural limits, and realigning purpose, identity, vision, values, strategy, and structure with where your organization is going next. Whether you are at the idea stage or years into operation, the question remains the same: *Is your organization designed for where it is going — or only for where it started?* That is where Chapter 1 begins.

Chapter 1
Define the Problem, Purpose, & Possibility

"The key to success is to start before you are ready, but not before you are clear." **Marie Forleo**, Life Coach and Entrepreneur

Know the need. Clarify the why. Articulate the mission. Envision what only you can build.

B efore you can build an organization that scales, you must first understand what you are truly building for. Many founders rush into action. They form entities, launch offerings, and chase early traction without fully understanding the problem they are trying to solve. They brainstorm solutions, test ideas, and move fast. But they skip the most important step: *clarity*. Clarity begins with slowing down long enough to ask better questions.

Early in my work with founders, I noticed that most growth challenges were not caused by lack of effort or intelligence. They were caused by misdiagnosis. Founders were solving visible symptoms rather than the underlying problem. They built features, expanded services, and hired more people, yet progress stalled.

One moment crystallized this for me. I was working with a founder whose company had steady demand but stagnant growth. Revenue was flat. The team was exhausted. The founder believed the issue was marketing. When we stepped back and examined the business, something else emerged. The problem was not demand. It was focus. The organization was trying to solve too many problems for too many people, all at once.

Once the real problem became clear, everything else followed. Positioning sharpened. Decisions simplified. Growth resumed. That experience reinforced a pattern I have seen repeatedly: **organizations struggle not because they lack solutions, but because they are unclear about the problem they exist to solve.** This chapter exists to help you avoid that mistake.

Before you design an identity, choose a structure, or think about scale, you must first define the problem, clarify your purpose, and understand what is possible if you solve that problem well. That is where all durable organizations begin. We start with the most important question of all: *What problem are you truly solving - and is it worth scaling?*

1.1. Problem You Solve, Need You Meet, Gap You Bridge

Some founders begin with a clearly defined problem. Others begin with something less precise but equally real — a gap, a friction, a need that is not being met as well as it should be. People are underserved. Systems are misaligned. Value is being lost.

What draws founders in is often instinctive before it becomes analytical. The trouble begins later, when that original impulse is forced into a narrow "problem-solving" frame. <u>Needs get reduced to features. Gaps get mistaken for tactics. Momentum replaces meaning.</u>

Organizations that last are not built merely to fix isolated problems. They are designed to meet enduring needs and bridge meaningful gaps over time. *Scale to Last* begins by restoring this distinction — between the problem you think you are solving and the deeper need your organization must be structured to serve.

Why Narrow Problem Definitions Limit Scale

Much conventional advice tells founders not to build unless the market can clearly articulate the problem. History suggests otherwise. As **Steve Jobs** famously observed, <u>customers often don't know what they want until you show it to them.</u> His point was not to ignore people, but to recognize that meaningful innovation often begins with conviction — before validation.

Purpose-driven organizations are built the same way. Founders must believe in the value of what they are creating even when the need is not yet fully visible. Data refines direction; it does not replace belief. The risk is not conviction. The risk is unclear definition.

Speed Without Clarity Creates Fragility

Founders are constantly urged to move fast — launch quickly, test publicly, pivot aggressively. ***But speed without clarity does not create scale.*** It creates exposure. The issue is rarely lack of opportunity. It is misalignment — between the problem being addressed, the need being met, the gap being bridged, and the organization being built to do the work. When these drift apart, progress feels busy but brittle. <u>Scaling amplifies whatever already exists. Clarity compounds. Confusion spreads.</u>

Symptoms Are Not the Problem

Founders often mistake signals for root causes. A drop in sales is not the problem. Low engagement is not the problem. High churn is not the problem. These are indicators. The real issue usually lives beneath the surface — in *unclear value, misaligned positioning, or flawed assumptions about who the organization truly exists to serve.* Treating symptoms as problems leads to activity without direction.

I've seen founders respond to slowing momentum with more action — new offers, new marketing, new hires. Action feels responsible. Pausing feels risky. Yet when we slow down long enough to diagnose before prescribing, the issue is almost always definition, not execution. <u>Once the true problem, need, or gap is named clearly, solutions become simpler</u> — and far more effective.

Definition Determines Scale

Not all problems scale. Some create leverage. Others quietly trap organizations in complexity and founder dependence. Scalable challenges tend to be persistent, shared by many, costly enough to justify action, and solvable through systems rather than constant customization. This distinction matters because scale magnifies everything — alignment or drift, focus or noise.

How you define what you exist to solve, serve, and bridge shapes everything that follow: positioning, business model, pricing, hiring, systems, and exit options. <u>This is not a branding exercise. It is a strategic decision.</u> Before you build further, you must be able to answer clearly:

- What problem are we addressing?
- Which needs are we meeting?
- Which gaps are we intentionally bridging — and for whom?

Clarity here does not slow you down. It prevents years of correction later.

1.2 Founder Intent, Purpose, and Mission

Once clarity exists around the problem you are solving, the next question becomes unavoidable: ***Why this organization — and why you?*** Before an organization can articulate purpose or mission, a founder must understand their own intent. This step is often skipped.

Founders are trained to analyze markets and move quickly toward launch. When intent is unclear early, that ambiguity carries forward.

The organization may still grow — but growth feels heavier than it should. Decisions slow. Commitment weakens under pressure. <u>Founder intent is the unseen force behind early design choices.</u> Whether acknowledged or not, it shapes what receives attention, which tradeoffs feel acceptable, and which compromises quietly accumulate.

Purpose Begins With Orientation, Not Language

At this stage, purpose is not a statement. It is orientation. For some founders, *purpose is personal* — shaped by lived experience, conviction, or injustice they cannot ignore. For others, *it is pragmatic* — building something valuable, creating opportunity, or responding to clear demand. <u>Both paths are legitimate.</u>

What matters is not where purpose comes from, but whether it is examined honestly. When founders fail to examine intent, they often commit to paths that look promising externally but feel misaligned internally. Over time, *that misalignment shows up as fatigue, hesitation, or second-guessing* — especially as complexity increases.

Meaning Sustains What Motivation Cannot

Early momentum is often fueled by emotion — urgency, dissatisfaction, or the desire for independence. That energy can start a company. It cannot sustain one.

Viktor Frankl observed that people endure hardship not through motivation alone, but through meaning. The same applies to founders. Motivation fluctuates as markets tighten and responsibilities compound. Meaning provides continuity when conditions become unfavorable. Organizations anchored only in short-term success often stall once early momentum fades. Those anchored in meaning develop resilience and attract people who stay for contribution, not just compensation.

When Intent and Mission Drift Apart

Every organization eventually confronts the same question: *Why do we exist?* When the answer is weak, borrowed, or unclear, focus erodes. Decisions become reactive. Growth happens without coherence. The strongest alignment occurs when founder intent is reflected — fully or partially — in the organization's mission. This does not require idealism. Some organizations exist primarily to pursue opportunity efficiently. In those cases, perfect overlap is not required — **clarity is**. Problems arise when founders tell themselves one story while living another. This is not a character flaw. It is a design failure.

From Intent to Mission

Founder intent creates internal alignment. Mission translates that alignment into external direction. **Jim Collins and Jerry Porras** observed that enduring organizations anchored themselves in a stable core purpose while allowing strategies and offerings to evolve. Profit mattered — but it was treated as fuel, not the destination.

A mission answers a practical question: ***What are we here to do, for whom, and in what way?*** When intent is clear, mission becomes a decision filter. It guides priorities, anchors tradeoffs, and keeps growth coherent as the organization evolves. With clarity around the problem, the need, and the gap — and alignment between founder intent and organizational purpose — you are positioned to design an organization that can grow without losing itself.

1.3 When Purpose Meets Market Reality

Once founder intent is clear and purpose has been examined honestly, the work shifts from internal alignment to external reality.

Clarity alone is not enough. An organization may feel meaningful and well-intentioned — and still fail to survive.

The market does not evaluate purpose. It responds to behavior. It reveals whether a problem is felt strongly enough, whether a need is urgent enough, and whether a gap is valuable enough to sustain action.

Where Missions Break Down

I've worked with founders who were deeply committed to what they were building. The problem was real. The intent was sincere. Yet the organization struggled — not because the mission lacked value, but because it lacked support. People agreed with the cause. They praised the idea. They nodded in conversations. But they did not invest — not consistently, not enough, and not in ways that allowed the work to endure. *Agreement is not demand. Appreciation is not funding.*

The Test Every Purpose Must Pass

Every organization eventually faces a practical question: ***who is willing to support this work — and how?*** Support may come through money, time, attention, access, or influence. But it must come reliably. Without it, even meaningful missions become fragile.

I've seen founders burn themselves out carrying work that was never designed to sustain itself. Passion turned into pressure. Sacrifice became expectation. Fulfillment gave way to exhaustion. This does not diminish purpose. It disciplines it.

Funding Is Stewardship, Not Compromise

One of the most damaging beliefs founders carry is that economics compromise meaning. In reality, economics determine whether meaning can endure. Funding is not a betrayal of purpose. It is stewardship. Sometimes this means narrowing the scope.

Sometimes, redefining the customer. Sometimes, choosing a model that supports the mission indirectly rather than forcing monetization where it does not belong.

Not every purpose is meant to be monetized directly. Some businesses exist to fund missions. Others embed missions within commercial models. Clarity here protects both.

When Alignment Beats Independence

Another truth founders often resist: *you do not have to build everything alone.* There are moments when the problem is real, and the gap is clear — but the infrastructure, experience, or capital required to scale responsibly is not yet present. In those moments, partnership or alignment with existing organizations may be the wiser move. This is not failure. It is strategic humility.

Many missions endure not because one founder carried them alone, but because they were embedded within systems designed to support them.

Holding Conviction and Reality Together

Strong founders hold two forces at once. They refuse to abandon what matters — and they refuse to ignore what is true. They test assumptions. They watch behavior. They allow evidence to refine conviction without eroding intent.

When purpose, need, gap, and market support align, an organization gains the ability not just to start — but to last. That alignment is not discovered through belief alone. It is designed, tested, and reinforced in the real world.

1.4 Form, Acquire, or Partner: Each Locks in Different Risks

Once needs are confirmed, gaps are understood, and funding paths are realistic, the next question becomes unavoidable: *what is the smartest way to enter this space?*

- Do you build from scratch?
- Do you buy something that already exists?
- Or do you align with others instead of going it alone?

This decision shapes everything that follows. Experienced founders and investors treat it as a *primary design choice*, not an afterthought.

Why "Build by Default" Is Risky

Most founders instinctively want to build. Starting from zero feels creative, independent, and personal. That instinct is understandable — but instinct alone is not strategy. Building means no customers, no operating history, no proven systems, and no predictable cash flow. <u>Decades of data show that most startups fail not because the ideas were bad, but because execution risk, capital strain, timing, and founder fatigue compound quickly.</u>

Buying changes the equation. Customers exist. Revenue is visible. Systems can be evaluated. Problems are known. *You are no longer betting on whether a model works* — only whether it can work better. That is a fundamentally different risk profile.

Control vs Leverage

Building offers clean design and control — but demands time, resilience, and tolerance for uncertainty. Buying offers leverage — momentum, data, and infrastructure — along with inherited complexity. <u>Neither path is superior by default.</u>

Building often makes sense when the problem is new, differentiation requires a fresh start, or capital is limited but time is available. Buying tends to make sense when demand already exists, speed matters, or cash flow is needed to fund growth. *The mistake is assuming one path fits every founder.*

Buying Is Not Avoiding Work

Acquisition is rarely passive. In practice, it is often the beginning of redesign. Strong operators keep what works and change what does not. They refine systems, strengthen culture, reposition offerings, and prepare the organization for its next stage.

Many struggling companies become strong not because they were rebuilt from scratch, but because they were acquired by someone better equipped to lead them. Buying is not about doing less work. It is about choosing **where** to do the work.

The Most Overlooked Path: Partnership

A third option is often underestimated: *alignment.* Many organizations scale not because of a single founder, but because complementary capabilities came together early — vision with operations, product with distribution, strategy with execution. <u>The right partnership can compress years of learning and reduce blind spots.</u> The wrong one can destroy momentum. Choosing a partner is not a relationship decision. It is a *design decision*.

Choose Intentionally

Sometimes the smartest move is to build. Sometimes it is to buy. Sometimes it is to partner, join, or embed within an existing platform. What matters is not the path you choose — but that you choose it deliberately. This decision affects speed, capital requirements, leadership demands, scalability, valuation, and exit options. That is why it belongs in the design phase, not after launch.

Whether you form, acquire, or align, the principles in this book remain the same: Design matters. Intent matters. Structure matters. Stability matters. Scale matters. Exit matters. This book is not about how you enter the journey. It is about how you design it to last.

Reflect & Practice

Reflection Prompts

- What problem, need, or gap is this organization truly designed to serve — beyond the initial idea?
- Where might I be defaulting to speed, control, or familiarity instead of strategy?
- Which entry path best aligns with the scale, risk, and exit outcomes I want?

Practice Challenge (7 Days)

For the next week:

1. Write one clear paragraph answering: *Should this be built, bought, or partnered — and why?*
2. Identify the primary risk you would assume under each option.
3. Choose the path that reduces long-term dependency, not just short-term discomfort.

Clarity at the beginning does not slow you down. It prevents years of structural regret later.

Chapter 2
Design Organization Identity & Business Model

"Your business model is your story of how you intend to create and deliver value." **Alexander Osterwalder**, Business Theorist and Author

Shape identity. Position with intention. Craft offers that matter. Build a model that sustains.

C larity about the problem is essential, and alignment of purpose is foundational. But neither becomes real until it takes form. Ideas do not scale. Intent does not scale. ***Design does.*** Once founders move beyond the question "What problem are we solving?" the more consequential question emerges: *What kind of organization must exist to solve it well and sustain it at scale?* This is where many ventures begin to drift.

I have worked with founders who were deeply committed to their mission and clear about the problem they were addressing yet still struggled to grow sustainably. The issue was rarely effort, intelligence, or passion. More often, their organizational identity was vague, and their business model evolved by default rather than by design. They were building momentum without a blueprint.

When Identity Is Unclear, Everything Else Suffers

Organizations express identity whether founders define it or not. When identity remains unclear, positioning becomes reactive, offerings multiply without coherence, teams pull in different directions, customers struggle to articulate the value, and growth introduces confusion rather than momentum. Decisions increase, but alignment weakens.

By contrast, when identity is intentionally designed, decisions simplify. Tradeoffs become clearer. The organization develops a recognizable center of gravity that guides behavior, communication, and priorities internally and externally.

Identity is not branding. It is not a logo, tagline, or marketing message. Identity answers a deeper question: *Who are we, really, and why should anyone care?* When founders cannot answer that clearly, neither can their teams nor their customers.

The Hidden Cost of an Accidental Business Model

Many founders treat the business model as a secondary concern. Pricing is postponed, revenue streams emerge organically, and assumptions go untested. This may work in the early stages, but it becomes dangerous as complexity increases. An accidental business model creates invisible strain: revenue that does not match effort, growth that outpaces systems, offerings that sell but do not sustain, and increasing dependence on the founder to hold everything together. Over time, the organization works harder to achieve diminishing returns.

A designed business model, by contrast, tells a coherent story of how value is created, delivered, and sustained. It aligns purpose with economics and vision with execution, allowing the organization to grow without requiring the founder to be everywhere at once.

Design Is Where Scale Becomes Possible

This chapter is not about logos, taglines, or surface-level strategy. It is about shaping the core architecture of the organization: who it exists for, what it offers, and how it operates in the real world. Design turns clarity into structure.

Founders who skip this work may still grow, but growth magnifies confusion. Founders who engage it intentionally build organizations that can scale, adapt, and eventually transfer value beyond themselves. ***Design is the bridge between intention and impact.***

With the foundation set in Chapter 1, we are now in Chapter 2, moving from *why* to *how* - designing an organization capable of carrying purpose, delivering value, and sustaining growth. That work begins with mission, vision, and values.

2.1 Mission, Vision, Values

Most organizations struggle to scale not because they lack talent, funding, or opportunity, but because they were never clear about who they were meant to be.

- Before systems break, culture cracks;
- Before culture cracks, alignment erodes; and
- Before alignment erodes, mission, vision, and values were unclear, borrowed, or ignored.

This is not a branding issue. It is a design failure.

Mission, vision, and values form the internal architecture of an organization. They shape decisions long before strategy does. When designed intentionally, they act as filters for judgment, behavior, and tradeoffs. When left vague, they become liabilities that quietly weaken alignment as complexity increases.

I have seen strong organizations unravel after a single hiring or partnership decision, not because of incompetence, but because there was no shared standard to evaluate fit or name misalignment early. This is precisely what mission, vision, and values are meant to prevent.

Mission Moves; Vision Sees; Values Guard

One of the most common mistakes founders make is treating mission and vision as interchangeable statements meant to sound inspiring. They are not the same. *Mission is directional*; it defines why the organization exists and the work it is committed to doing. *Vision is visual*; it describes what the world looks like when the mission succeeds. If mission is a verb, vision is a picture. When founders blur the two, organizations stay busy without direction, and growth becomes reactive rather than intentional.

The problem compounds when the mission and the vision are borrowed from other companies. Language that is inherited rather than discovered rarely produces commitment. <u>People sense when words are performative</u>, which is why so many statements live on websites but never show up in decisions.

Values Are Not Aspirations; They Are Standards

Values are often misunderstood as ideals or personality traits. In practice, they serve a strategic role. Values act as guardians: they protect the mission from compromise, the vision from distortion, and the organization from slow cultural decay. *Well-designed values reinforce what truly matters, clarify who belongs and who does not, and anchor decisions as complexity increases.*

For this reason, values should not be selected casually or retrofitted later. I do not help founders choose values; I help them discover them. Values should emerge from the problem being solved, the behaviors required to solve it well, and the kind of leadership needed to sustain the vision. When discovered this way:

1. Values become operational,
2. Guiding hiring, promotion, partnerships, and
3. Exits.

Without this clarity, culture becomes accidental, and accidental cultures rarely scale.

Why This Matters for Scale and Exit

Scale amplifies everything: clarity or confusion, alignment or dysfunction, values or their absence. Organizations that struggle to scale often realize too late that growth was built on a fragile identity. Founders become bottlenecks, decisions slow, culture fragments, and buyers see risk instead of value.

Strong mission, vision, and values do not guarantee success, but weak ones almost guarantee struggle, and they directly affect:

- Leadership distribution,
- Decision speed,
- Cultural consistency,
- Valuation confidence, and
- Transferability beyond the founder.

Identity design is not philosophical work; it is strategic and structural.

Founder Alignment Comes First

Before mission, vision, and values are articulated outwardly, they must be clarified inwardly. Founders bring intent, beliefs, motivations, and blind spots into the organization, whether consciously or not. When founder intent is examined and aligned, organizations gain coherence; when it is ignored, organizations inherit confusion. *Alignment does not require shared worldviews, but it does require honesty about why the organization exists and what it is meant to become.* When intent is clear, decisions simplify, leadership matures, culture stabilizes, and scale becomes intentional.

Internal alignment, however, is only half the work. Identity must translate outward. If mission, vision, and values are real, they should shape not only how the organization operates, but how it shows up for the people it exists to serve.

The Customer Is the Hero—Not the Organization

As Donald Miller explains in *Building a StoryBrand*, organizations lose clarity when they position themselves as the hero of the story. Customers are not looking for impressive companies to admire; they are looking for guides who understand their struggle and can help them move forward. When organizations center themselves, messaging becomes abstract and inward-looking. When the customer is placed at the center, positioning sharpens, and the organization's role becomes clear: to guide, support, and equip the customer to succeed.

This connects directly to identity. <u>Mission, vision, and values are not only internal anchors; they shape how the organization shows up in the marketplace.</u> When identity aligns with the customer's journey, positioning stops being performative. Marketing simplifies, sales conversations feel natural, and growth becomes aligned rather than forced. That is how identity turns into traction.

2.2 Target Groups and Positioning

One of the earliest and most uncomfortable decisions founders face is deciding who the organization is actually for. Many avoid answering this directly, opting instead for broad statements such as "we serve anyone who needs this" or "our product applies to everyone." While understandable, this instinct is dangerous. Organizations that attempt to speak to everyone usually end up resonating with no one.

As Seth Godin reminds us, meaningful organizations are built around tribes - specific groups of people connected by shared beliefs, needs, and aspirations. Scale does not come from widening the net, but from deepening resonance. <u>Clarity of audience is not a marketing constraint; it is a strategic commitment.</u>

Know Your Primary Audience Before You Multiply Offerings

Customers do not want to be impressed; they want to feel understood. That begins with clarity about who the organization exists to serve. Every organization should be able to name its primary audience - the group it understands best - and, where relevant, identify secondary audiences served intentionally through distinct offers.

Some organizations successfully serve multiple segments, but they do so deliberately. *Automotive brands like Toyota manage this by treating each segment as its own ecosystem, not by blending audiences together.* Problems arise when audiences blur: messaging dilutes, offers lose focus, and teams struggle to prioritize. Clarity about the primary audience is not limiting; it simplifies decisions and strengthens alignment.

Positioning Is About Role, Not Ego

Positioning is often misunderstood as self-promotion. In reality, it is about role clarity. Strong positioning answers four essential questions:

- Who this is for,
- What problem they are facing,
- Why they should trust the organization, and
- What outcome they can reasonably expect.

When these answers are clear, positioning feels natural rather than forced.

Influence, Remarkability, and Meaning

In *Key Person of Influence*, Daniel Priestley explains that influence is designed, not accidental. It grows through clarity of message and consistency of contribution. Visibility creates opportunity only when it is anchored in understanding. Similarly, Seth Godin makes a blunt point: in crowded markets, being competent is no longer enough. Blending in is invisible. Remarkable does not mean loud; it means specific and meaningful to the right audience.

The strongest organizations do not chase attention broadly. They choose a tribe and serve it exceptionally well.

1. When target groups are vague, positioning becomes generic.
2. When target groups are clear, positioning becomes obvious.

Differentiation Does Not Require Reinvention

Differentiation does not always come from doing something entirely new. Many organizations stand out by doing familiar things differently - through delivery, experience, storytelling, systems, or values-driven positioning. In some cases, the distinction lies in who the work is for; in others, how it is done or why it exists. Innovation is not limited to products. It can emerge through perspective.

People do not follow products; they follow meaning. Organizations that help people feel seen and aligned around something that matters create loyalty, not just transactions. Scale follows belonging, not breadth.

Generalist or Specialist: A Conscious Choice

There is no universal rule about being a specialist or a generalist. Both paths work, and both fail when chosen unconsciously. Specialists often scale faster early because their message is sharp. Generalists, as explored in **Range** and by thinkers like **Alan Weiss**, often integrate broader patterns and build long-term value. The mistake is not choosing one path over the other; it is drifting into a position by default.

Alignment Between Identity and Audience

Target groups must align with the organization's mission, vision, and values. *When alignment is strong, marketing feels natural, hiring simplifies, partnerships make sense, and growth compounds.* When alignment is weak, everything feels forced, and scale amplifies friction rather than clarity.

Once the target group is clear, the value proposition stops being abstract. Whether framed as a UVP, USP, or FAB, the objective is the same: clearly articulate why this audience should care. Strong value propositions are not designed to impress everyone. They are designed to resonate deeply with the right people. This is where identity meets market reality.

2.3 Offer Design and Early Value Proposition

Ideas do not scale. ***Offers do.*** One of the most common gaps in early-stage organizations is this: founders are clear about purpose and thoughtful about positioning, yet vague about what they are actually offering. They speak about services or solutions but struggle to answer a basic question: *What exactly are people buying?*

Organizations do not scale on intention. They scale on offers. An offer is the practical expression of value in the market where identity meets decision-making. In early stages, offers do more than generate revenue. They reveal who the audience truly is and what they are willing to commit to.

Offers Are Designed, Not Discovered

In *$100M Offers*, Alex Hormozi argues that most businesses do not struggle because their product is weak, but because their offer is unclear or misaligned. Value exists, but it is often packaged poorly. A strong offer makes value unmistakable by doing four things:

- Clarifies the outcome
- Reduces perceived risk
- Simplifies the decision
- Makes the value obvious

Founders often assume customers will "figure it out." They won't. Confusion is friction, and friction kills momentum. That is why offer design is strategic work, not marketing polish.

An Offer Is More Than a Product or Service

An offer is not just what you sell. It is a bundle of decisions that answers, implicitly or explicitly:

- Who this is for
- What problem it solves
- What outcome it promises
- What commitment it requires

As marketing and sales professionals consistently observe, people do not buy products. They buy outcomes they believe are worth the cost and risk. When offers fail, it is rarely because the solution lacks merit; it is because the offer lacks clarity or urgency. Early offers must answer one question clearly: *Why should someone say yes now?*

Value Is Created by Perception, Not Price

"People do not buy features. They buy outcomes." Effective offers combine a clear problem, a specific promise, reduced risk, and a believable path to results. This is why two organizations can sell similar services at very different prices, and both succeed. The difference is not cost. It is clarity. When offers are designed intentionally, founders stop competing on price and start competing on relevance.

Front-End, Back-End, and the Path of Commitment

Russell Brunson highlights a critical distinction: not all offers serve the same role. Some introduce people to your world, some deepen trust and transformation, and others deliver speed, access, or leverage. Problems arise when founders push high-commitment offers before trust exists, or underprice transformational work and burn out. As many high-ticket practitioners emphasize, high-ticket is not about charging more; it is about delivering clearer value to a narrower audience. <u>Offer structure quietly determines who enters your ecosystem and how seriously they engage.</u>

Your Offers Shape Your Audience

Audience selection happens through offers, not messaging alone. Low-commitment offers attract one type of buyer; high-commitment offers attract another. ***Offer design filters seriousness, readiness, expectations, and behavior.*** When offers align with positioning and mission, growth flows. When they do not, friction multiplies.

Early Value Proposition: Clarity Before Sophistication

Early value propositions fail because founders try to sound impressive instead of being clear. Strong early value propositions do three things well:

- Focus on one primary problem
- Promise one clear outcome
- Remove unnecessary friction

Sophistication can come later. Confusion is costly early.

From Incremental Growth to Durable Advantage

In *Zero to One*, Peter Thiel argues that lasting companies are built by creating value that is difficult to copy. Scale rewards uniqueness more than effort. If an offer does not create a defensible advantage, growth accelerates competition rather than value. Early offers should therefore test not only demand, but distinctiveness.

Offers as Learning Tools, Not Final Answers

Early offers are not final answers. They are experiments with intent. Each offer teaches founders what people value, what they resist, and what they are willing to commit to. Founders who treat early offers as fixed stall. Those who treat them as learning tools evolve faster.

Customers enter at different levels of awareness, trust, and readiness. Effective organizations design sequences that allow people to start where they are and move forward over time. Scaling organizations do not push customers forward. *They lead them forward.*

2.4 Business Model Essentials (pricing, revenue models, assumptions)

Purpose gives direction. Positioning creates clarity. Offers express value. *But the business model determines whether the organization survives long enough to matter.* Offers reveal what people are willing to commit to; business models determine whether that commitment can be sustained, scaled, and transferred.

At its core, a business model answers a simple, unforgiving question: *How does this organization make money in a way that is repeatable, sustainable, and aligned with who it is?* Not someday. Not hypothetically. In reality.

Business Models Are Choices, Not Defaults

Many founders never consciously choose a business model; they inherit one. Early revenue often comes from what is easiest to sell - hourly services, one-off projects, or custom work. Over time, the organization becomes trapped inside a model it never designed. Every model carries tradeoffs: some scale through volume, others through leverage, margin, or repetition. The mistake is not choosing the "wrong" model; it is choosing one unintentionally.

The Business Model Is the Logic Behind the Mission

In *Business Model Generation*, Alexander Osterwalder defines a business model as the logic of how an organization creates, delivers, and captures value. This matters because when the model is unclear, effort increases, complexity rises, and profitability lags. A well-designed model aligns mission with economics. Solving the problem you care about must also be how the organization sustains itself. Sustainability is not accidental. When the model fails to support the mission, the mission eventually suffers.

There Is No Single Right Model—Only the Right Fit

Organizations thrive using very different models: product-based, service-based, subscription, licensing, franchising, or hybrid approaches. **Walmart** wins through scale and efficiency. Luxury brands win through identity and scarcity. Both succeed because the model matches who they serve. Problems arise when founders mix models without coherence or chase trends instead of alignment.

Delivery Is Strategic, Not Operational

How value is delivered is a strategic choice, not a logistical detail. Physical models often build trust but carry higher fixed costs. Digital models offer reach but demand clarity and systems. Hybrid models combine both. What matters is alignment with the audience served, the value delivered, the margins required, and the scale or exit envisioned.

The Model Must Match the Identity

Mission, vision, values, and positioning should guide the business model - not the other way around. Two questions matter most: *Does this model support the organization we want to build?* And *can it function without constant founder involvement?* If the answer is no, the model may generate revenue, but it will resist scale.

Profitability Enables Purpose

Profitability is not greed; it is oxygen. Without it, pressure rises, decisions become reactive, and exit options shrink. A model that cannot fund the organization will eventually undermine purpose, people, and value.

Models That Scale Reduce Founder Dependence

Scalable models create value without requiring the founder to be everywhere. When systems carry the load, growth and exit become possible. Buyers do not acquire effort; they acquire systems.

Design for Sustainability Before Optimization

At this stage, the goal is not optimization but coherence. A strong early model is simple enough to understand, consistent enough to repeat, and stable enough to fund operations. Optimization comes later. Sustainability comes first.

From Model to Momentum

Identity informs positioning. Positioning shapes offers. Offers feed the business model. Together, they create an organization capable of growth without self-destruction.

Reflect & Practice

Reflection Prompts

- Is our **mission, vision, and values** actually guiding decisions — or are they decorative statements?
- Who is this organization truly for — and where might our positioning or offers be trying to serve too many audiences at once?
- What business model are we operating today — and did we design it intentionally, or inherit it by default?

Practice Challenge (7 Days)

For the next week:

1. Write one paragraph that clearly connects identity, audience, offer, and revenue into a single, coherent story.
2. Map your current business model on one page (who pays, for what, how often, and why).
3. Identify one assumption — about positioning, pricing, demand, or delivery — that has never been tested, and pressure-test it with a trusted advisor or partner.

A business model does not need to be perfect. But identity, positioning, offers, and economics must align.

You have now completed the ***design phase***. Next, we move from intention to implementation — forming the organization that will carry out what you have designed.

Chapter 3
Choose the Right Structure & Strategic Vehicle

"Your structure must support your strategy, or your strategy will fall apart."
Michael Porter, Businessman and Professor

Choose wisely. Align structure with vision. Select the right path. Build for tomorrow, not just today.

By this point, you have clarity about the problem you are solving, the purpose driving the organization, the audience you serve, the value you offer, and the model that sustains it. Now comes a quieter — but far more consequential — decision: *What structure will carry all of this forward?* Before an organization can stabilize, scale, or exit, it must be able to stand.

Structure Is Not Paperwork

Many founders treat structure as an administrative formality — something to "get out of the way" so they can start operating. But structure is not paperwork. It is not compliance. And it is not a box to check on the way to launch. Structure is architecture. It determines:

- How decisions are made
- How power and ownership are distributed
- How risk is absorbed
- How capital flows
- How easily the organization can grow, partner, or exit

Why Structure Fails Later, Not Sooner

Poorly chosen structures rarely fail immediately. They fail later —
when growth introduces friction, when investors ask harder
questions, or when founders attempt to step back and discover they
cannot.

I have seen founders build compelling brands and strong offers,
only to realize too late that *their legal structure restricted growth, their
ownership model created conflict, or their chosen path made investment or exit
unattractive.* By the time they noticed, change was costly, painful, and
sometimes irreversible.

Choosing for Tomorrow, Not Just Today

This chapter exists to help you slow down before those costs
appear. It helps you choose the right structure and strategic vehicle.
This task is not about optimizing for speed TODAY. It is about
building something that can adapt, scale, and eventually outgrow
you — without collapsing.

That is the work ahead.

3.1 Legal Structures & Organizational Structure

Structure shapes behavior long before it shapes outcomes. Legal
structure is often treated as a technical or compliance decision, yet
in practice, it influences how founders think about risk,
compensation, ownership, and control. What appears to be a tax
decision on paper becomes a leadership and scalability issue under
pressure.

Structure does not sit quietly in the background; it determines how
decisions are made when things get hard.

Structure Must Serve Strategy—Not the Other Way Around

In *Competitive Strategy*, **Michael Porter** argues that advantage comes not from activity alone, but from alignment. Strategy defines how an organization intends to compete. Structure determines whether that strategy can actually be executed. When structure is chosen without strategy, organizations drift into contradiction: people are held accountable without authority, incentives conflict, and growth introduces friction instead of leverage.

You do not choose structure to get started; you choose structure to support where the organization is going. The wrong structure can neutralize a strong strategy. The right one amplifies it.

Common Legal Structures—and Why They Exist

Legal structures exist to serve different organizational realities. There is no universally "best" structure—only one that fits, or one that quietly works against you.

- **LLCs** offer flexibility and simplicity, making them useful in early stages where experimentation matters.
- **S-Corps** introduce payroll discipline and tax structure once cash flow stabilizes.
- **C-Corps** are built for scale, outside capital, and complex ownership, but bring rigidity and investor expectations.
- **Nonprofits and mission-driven entities** prioritize purpose over profit and require clarity and discipline from the start.
- **Trusts and holding structures** support asset protection, long-term ownership, or succession rather than daily operations.

The cost of choosing too quickly is real. ***Structures selected for convenience, peer advice, or speed often become expensive*** to change later due to tax consequences, ownership disputes, compliance complexity, or investor hesitation. The better question is not what is easiest to start, but what can support where the organization is going.

Structure Is How Strategy Becomes Operable

Organizational structure is often reduced to charts and titles, but its real function is operational. Structure determines how decisions travel, how information flows, and how accountability holds as complexity increases. A clear mission without structure becomes aspiration. A sound strategy without structure becomes frustrating. Structure is not neutral; it either accelerates execution or quietly obstructs it.

Well-aligned structures clarify ownership, enable coordination, and make expectations visible. Misaligned structures blur authority, slow work, and drain energy—even in talented organizations.

Common Organizational Design Choices

There is no single best organizational design, only designs that fit the work being done. Most organizations use one of the following, or a hybrid, as they scale:

1. **Hierarchical structures** emphasize clarity, discipline, and risk control; they're effective in regulated or operationally complex environments.
2. **Functional structures** group work by expertise, improving efficiency but slowing cross-functional coordination at scale.
3. **Flat structures** reduce layers and increase autonomy, supporting speed and innovation while relying on trust and maturity.
4. **Matrix structures** balance multiple priorities across functions, products, or regions, demanding strong communication and clear decision rights.
5. **Project-based or ad hoc structures** organize around initiatives or clients, enabling adaptability but requiring tight accountability.
6. **Hybrid structures** combine elements of the above and are increasingly common as organizations grow.

The mistake is not choosing the wrong structure. **The mistake is choosing by default instead of by design.**

3.2 Governance & Ownership Models

Ownership answers a fundamental question: *Who controls the future?* Governance and ownership are not merely legal topics; they define power. They determine who decides, who benefits, who carries risk, and who has a voice when things get difficult. Many early conflicts inside organizations are not personality problems but governance problems that were never clarified.

Common Ownership Pitfalls

Some of the most common issues include:

- Equal ownership without equal contribution
- Undefined decision rights
- Silent partners with loud opinions
- Founders unclear on final authority
- No plan for exits, buyouts, or succession

These issues often remain hidden when things are going well and surface quickly under stress.

Governance Is a Design Choice, Not a Reaction

Good governance does not slow organizations down; it prevents chaos. Clear governance answers critical questions:

- Who decides when there is disagreement?
- What happens if a founder steps back?
- How are disputes resolved?
- Who communicates during crises?
- How are new partners brought in or removed?

Founders who avoid these conversations early are often forced into them later—under far worse conditions.

3.3. Strategic Vehicles (start from scratch, acquire, franchise, license)

In Chapter 1, we explored whether to build, buy, or partner as entry decisions. Here, we return to those options as *strategic vehicles*, because how an organization enters or expands determines how it must be formed, governed, and scaled.

Building is not the only path, though many founders treat it as the default. Building, acquiring, franchising, and licensing are all vehicles for creating or extending market presence. Each carries distinct implications for control, capital, speed, complexity, and long-term optionality.

Why Smart Operators Often Buy Instead of Build

Experienced operators often prefer acquisition because it reduces uncertainty. Buying an existing organization can provide:

- Proven demand
- Established customers
- Operating systems
- Trained teams
- Immediate cash flow

This does not eliminate risk, but it changes its nature. Rather than testing whether a model works, you focus on improving one that already does.

Building from scratch offers control and creative freedom. Buying offers speed and validation. Franchising and licensing provide leverage, but introduce constraints around autonomy, consistency, and design. Each vehicle trades freedom for speed, or control for scale.

Vehicle Choice Shapes Everything That Follows

The strategic vehicle selected influences:

- Capital requirements
- Operational complexity
- Leadership demands
- Scalability
- Exit options

This is not a tactical decision; it is a directional one. The right vehicle depends on risk tolerance, access to capital, desired timeline, operating role, and long-term vision for ownership and exit. Founders who choose to intentionally design with leverage. Those who choose by default inherit constraints they later struggle to undo.

Strategic Vehicles as Design Decisions

Vehicle choice is not about ego or identity; it is about fit. Some organizations are best built. Others are best bought. Some scale fastest through franchising, licensing, or partnership. *The question is not which option sounds most impressive, but which supports the structure, governance, and scale you are designing.*

In the next section, we examine how these structural choices reveal themselves under pressure, and how scalability, transferability, and investor readiness expose whether an organization has truly been designed to last.

3.4 Scalability & Investor Readiness Considerations

Scale exposes weak structure. *Growth does not create problems; it reveals them.* As organizations expand, informal agreements break down, founder chivalry stop working, systems are tested, and culture is stressed. Structures that worked at a small scale often become liabilities at a larger one. This is where design decisions stop being theoretical and start being tested.

What Investors and Buyers Actually Look For

While financial performance matters, experienced investors and acquirers look beyond results. They assess risk embedded in the structure itself, including:

- Clarity of ownership
- Disciplined decision-making
- Leadership independence from the founder
- Governance maturity
- Structural flexibility

They are not just buying performance; they are buying risk—or avoiding it. *An organization can be profitable and still unattractive if authority, knowledge, or execution is concentrated in too few hands.*

Designing for Transferability

Organizations that exit well share a common trait: they can function without the founder at the center of everything. Structure makes this possible. <u>When designed intentionally, leadership becomes distributable, decisions repeatable, and value transferable.</u> When it is not, exits are discounted, delayed, or impossible. Transferability is not about removing the founder; it is about reducing dependency.

Reflect & Practice

Reflection Prompts

- Which structural decisions in this chapter (legal form, governance, ownership, vehicle choice) have I made by default rather than by design?
- Where might my current structure create friction, confusion, or founder dependence as the organization scales?
- If an investor or acquirer evaluated this organization today, what structural risks would stand out first?

Practice Challenge (7 Days)

For the next week:

1. List the key structural choices already made (entity type, ownership logic, governance approach, growth vehicle).
2. Identify one structural decision that directly affects scalability or exit readiness and deserves redesign.
3. Have one focused conversation with a qualified advisor (legal, financial, or strategic) to stress-test that decision against where the organization is headed.

Structure does not need to be perfect. *But it must be intentional.*

From Design to Formation

You have completed the design phase. Design creates clarity, but clarity alone does not build organizations.

Part II moves from intention to execution—forming what you have designed.

PART II

FORM & LEGALIZE

"The foundation of every enduring institution is built long before the world sees it." **James Clear**, Author and Performance Consultant

Document agreements. Establish systems. Form intentionally. Build a foundation that can carry growth.

Everyone has ideas. Some design thoughtfully. Very few form intentionally. Formation is where many promising ventures quietly undermine themselves.

Part I focused on design - clarifying purpose, identity, value, structure, and direction. But design alone does not create an organization. Until ideas are formalized into documents, agreements, systems, and roles, everything remains fragile. Formation is not just about compliance. It is about making purpose, ownership, authority, and accountability legally real — so the organization can scale, attract capital, and transfer value without renegotiating its foundations later.

Why Formation Is Where Many Founders Stumble

Most founders rush through formation, treating it as administrative, legal, or something to complete quickly so the "real work" can begin. That assumption is costly. Formation decisions quietly shape:

- Ownership and decision authority
- Information flow and reporting lines
- Conflict resolution and accountability
- Risk sharing and capital protection

Poor formation rarely causes immediate failure. Instead, it creates latent risk that surfaces later under pressure. *Many scaling struggles trace back not to a weak strategy, but to missing documents, unclear roles, informal agreements, or culture left to chance.*

Formation Turns Design Into Commitment

Design answers *what* and *why*. Formation answers *how*, *who*, and *under what rules*. This is where mission is documented, ownership is defined, expectations become enforceable, and culture is shaped intentionally. Without formation, organizations rely on goodwill, memory, and founder authority. That may work early. It does not survive growth. Formation institutionalizes trust rather than assuming it.

Why Formation Matters for Scale and Exit

Investors, partners, and acquirers rarely ask first about vision. They ask practical questions:

- Who owns the company?
- How are decisions made?
- Are agreements clear and enforceable?
- Can the organization operate without constant founder intervention?

Formation answers these questions long before exit discussions begin. Well-formed organizations scale with fewer surprises. Poorly formed ones accumulate friction, conflict, and valuation discounts. Exit does not fix weak formation. ***Exit exposes it.*** Even founders who plan to exit early set valuation here.

From Concept to Company

Part II focuses on the essential, often overlooked work that protects relationships, prevents conflict, clarifies expectations, creates operational trust, and increases enterprise value. This is where disciplined founders quietly gain advantage.

What You'll Build in Part II

In this part, you will learn how to:

- Translate vision into foundational documents
- Formalize strategy and operating logic
- Define ownership, governance, and authority
- Build early teams and advisory structures intentionally
- Shape culture before habits harden
- Form the organization legally and operationally with scale in mind

This is not bureaucracy. It is infrastructure.

A Note for Founders Who Have Already Started

Forming an organization is not a one-time event but an ongoing discipline. Many organizations are formed quickly or under pressure, and as they grow, early shortcuts become constraints. The chapters ahead help you revisit assumptions, strengthen agreements, clarify roles and authority, reduce hidden risks, and improve scalability and long-term value. Whether you are forming for the first time or reforming with hindsight, the question remains the same: is your organization built for where it is going, or only for where it started?

Chapter 4
Prepare the Foundational Documents

"If you don't document it, you don't own it." **Michael Gerber,** Author and Business Consultant

Document clearly. Protect legally. Formalize commitments. Turn vision into an organized entity.

Design clarifies what you want to build. **Formation determines whether it survives.** This chapter marks the shift from planning to commitment. Until now, most work has lived in conversations, concepts, and frameworks. From here forward, clarity must be captured, recorded, and enforced.

Foundational documents are where intentions stop being optional. They define how the organization operates when expectations collide, interests conflict, priorities compete, money is involved, relationships are tested, and growth introduces stress.

Many founders underestimate this stage because it feels uncreative or uncomfortable. Yet most organizational breakdowns stem not from bad intentions, but from *undocumented ones.*

Why Documents Matter More Than Most Founders Think

Founders often rely on optimism, saying:

- "We trust each other."
- "We'll figure it out as we go."
- "That feels too corporate for where we are."

These instincts are understandable, but incomplete. Documents are not about distrust; they are about clarity under pressure. They answer hard questions before emotions get involved:

- Who decides what?
- How are disagreements resolved?
- What does success look like?
- What happens if someone exits?
- How is the organization protected as it scales?

Without documentation, founders rely on assumptions. Assumptions hold in calm seasons and fail under stress.

Formation Is Where Risk Becomes Visible

Poor documentation rarely causes immediate failure. It creates a latent risk that surfaces later:

- When money enters
- When roles expand
- When performance diverges
- When delegation becomes necessary
- When external stakeholders demand clarity

I have seen strong relationships fracture not because of bad faith, but because nothing was clearly written down when alignment was strong. Foundational documents preserve alignment while it exists, so it can survive change.

Strategic Infrastructure, Not Legal Formality

This chapter is not about paperwork for its own sake. It focuses on the documents that matter most, why they exist, and how they support scale, governance, and exit. When done well, foundational documents:

- Reduce ambiguity

- Prevent conflict
- Accelerate decisions
- Increase investor confidence
- Strengthen valuation
- Protect relationships
- Make leadership distributable

When rushed or ignored, they quietly undermine everything else.

Before continuing, a mindset shift is required. Documents are not constraints; *they are containers.* They hold clarity, protect trust, and give the organization memory beyond the founder. If Part I helped you design wisely, Chapter 4 helps you commit responsibly. We begin with the document that aligns vision before anything else is built— this is where Section 4.1 begins.

4.1. Vision Impartation Document

Before an organization recruits board members, hires early leaders, or raises capital, it must answer one question clearly: **why it exists and where it is going.** The Vision Impartation Document (VID) exists for that purpose.

This is not a marketing or legal document. It is a founder's strategic reference used to transfer vision before influence, money, and decision-making authority expand. <u>Vision is not passed through enthusiasm alone; it must be articulated, documented, and shared intentionally.</u>

What the Vision Impartation Document Is

Founders carry vision intuitively; others do not. The VID translates what lives in the founder's mind into a shared frame that others can align with. It captures the organization's foundational logic, including:

- The core problem the organization exists to solve

- The mission, long-term vision, and direction
- Values, cultural standards, and leadership philosophy
- Strategic logic behind key choices
- Clients or beneficiaries being served
- Key economic and operating assumptions

Without this clarity, early supporters interpret the vision differently. Momentum may exist, but coherence does not.

How It Is Used in Practice

In practice, the VID functions as a single source of truth. I have used it and advised others to use it to:

- Anchor pitch decks for boards, advisors, and early sponsors
- Reinforce alignment after vision conversations
- Impart vision to early employees, volunteers, and key partners
- Onboard consultants and freelancers before they build anything
- Maintain consistency when multiple external parties are involved

Instead of explaining the organization in fragments and hoping alignment holds, the founder points to one intentional reference. *Misalignment, rework, and dilution drop sharply.*

Why This Document Matters

Most founders underestimate how little context external contributors have. Even skilled advisors are guessing without a clear understanding of the founder's vision, principles, and assumptions. The VID removes that risk.

It also protects continuity. If the founder steps back, exits, or becomes unavailable, the vision does not disappear. It is already captured. Direction is preserved. For investors and serious stakeholders, this signals maturity: the organization is not dependent on one person's memory or presence.

A Foundation, Not a Finish Line

The VID is not meant to be perfect or final. It is meant to be clear enough to align the right people early. It will evolve, but its role remains the same: **to preserve direction as complexity increases**. Once vision is imparted, the work shifts from clarity to execution. That is where we go next.

4.2. Strategic Plan & Business Plan

Vision inspires. *Plans stabilize.* Many founders carry a vision in their heads. That works—until it doesn't. I have seen organizations stall overnight when a founder became unavailable, not because the idea was weak, but because nothing had been written down. No one understood the long view or the logic behind decisions. Momentum collapsed. For investors, board members, and senior partners, this is an immediate red flag. If vision lives only in the founder's mind, the organization is fragile.

Why Vision Must Be Documented to Outlive the Founder

Peter Drucker argued in *The Practice of Management* that the role of management is clarity—turning intent into repeatable decisions. When vision is undocumented: decisions depend on proximity to the founder, leadership cannot be distributed, and strategy becomes interpretation rather than direction

Durable organizations institutionalize thinking. They translate vision into plans and systems that others can act on without constant explanation. If the founder steps away, the organization should not.

Strategic Plan First, Business Plan Second

Founders often jump straight to a business plan. That is a mistake. A **strategic plan** answers long-term questions:

- Where are we going over the next 3–5 years?
- What capabilities must we build?
- What tradeoffs are we willing to make?

Only then does a **business plan** make sense. Business plans are shorter-term and execution-focused:

1. Priorities, resources, and milestones
2. Revenue logic and cost structure

Without strategy, business plans become mechanical and reactive.

Scaling Through Disciplined Initiatives

In *The Road to a Billion*, Adam Coffey shows that scale comes from initiatives, not slogans. Organizations that scale:

- Assign clear ownership to initiatives
- Track progress relentlessly
- Review execution with the same rigor as financials

Strategy becomes scalable only when it is operationalized.

The Role of the Business Plan

A business plan is not just for attracting investors and lenders.
Its primary value is internal. A strong plan:

- Aligns priorities
- Clarifies assumptions and risks
- Defines metrics and milestones
- Guides resource allocation
- Creates accountability

It becomes the grounding reference when decisions need discipline.

Planning as Protection, Not Prediction

Plans do not predict the future. They prepare the organization to respond intelligently. Founders who avoid planning often claim flexibility, but the result is reactivity under pressure. Strategic and business plans create intentional optionality. With planning in place, the next step is formalizing the agreements, structures, and systems that allow execution. *That is where we go next.*

4.3. Operating Agreements, Bylaws, Shareholder Structures

This is where intent becomes enforceable. Up to this point, the work has been directional—vision clarified, strategy articulated, plans drafted. <u>Operating agreements and governance documents shift the organization from design to operation by defining how it actually functions under pressure, growth, money, and disagreement.</u> These are not planning documents; they are operating documents. They exist so decisions do not rely on memory, personality, or improvisation.

Every organization operates by design or by default. When governance documents are vague or missing, organizations default to informal power dynamics, personality-driven decisions, unclear authority, and inconsistent accountability. That may feel manageable early; it becomes dangerous as complexity increases. *Well-designed operating documents create order without micromanagement by clarifying decision rights, authority flow, dispute resolution, and ownership protections.* They translate vision and strategy into repeatable behavior.

What These Documents Govern

While formats vary by entity, operating agreements, bylaws, and ownership documents typically define decision authority, roles and responsibilities, governance and oversight mechanisms, ownership and equity logic, and boundaries that protect the organization under pressure. <u>These documents are not about control; they are about</u>

predictability, fairness, and continuity. A few pages here can prevent years of conflict later.

Entity Type Matters

Different entities require different governance mechanics:

- **LLCs** rely heavily on operating agreements to define authority, economics, and exits.
- **Corporations** require bylaws, shareholder agreements, and formal governance mechanics.
- **S-Corps** introduce ownership and compensation constraints that must be handled carefully.
- **Trusts and holding structures** emphasize control, succession, and asset protection more than daily operations.
- **Nonprofits** add fiduciary and regulatory obligations that demand clarity from day one.

The principle is consistent; implementation is not. This is why templates alone are rarely sufficient.

Use Professionals—Strategically

Because these documents are relied upon by regulators, investors, and courts, professional guidance matters. *Skilled advisors surface hidden risks, stress-test assumptions, align documents with strategy (not just compliance), structure ownership and compensation intelligently, and prevent costly corrections later.* This is not an area for improvisation or blind outsourcing.

The Team Charter: Governance at the Working Level

Beyond legal governance, teams need operational clarity. A Team Charter defines purpose, scope of authority, roles, resources, communication rhythms, and success metrics. Unlike legal documents, it governs how work gets done. It enables self-management, reduces escalation, and keeps execution aligned without constant founder intervention—governance where work actually happens.

Small Documents, Large Consequences

Though short, these agreements have an *outsized impact*: they prevent conflict, protect relationships, increase investor confidence, stabilize leadership transitions, and simplify exits. Structure does not eliminate tension; it keeps tension productive.

From Formation to Protection

Once operating agreements, governance structures, and team charters are in place, the organization becomes legible to regulators, investors, partners, and acquirers. The final layer of formation addresses compliance, permits, and intellectual property—the safeguards that protect what you are building as it enters the public, legal, and competitive environment. That is where we go next.

4.4. Compliance, Permits, IP Protection

Protect what you are building before the world touches it.

Early-stage organizations feel open and full of possibility — and that is exactly when they are most exposed. Compliance, permits, and intellectual property protection are often delayed because founders are busy building, selling, and surviving. The problem is simple: what you delay early often becomes what derails you later. *This section is not about turning you into a lawyer or accountant. It is about thinking like a serious builder.* Serious organizations do not only create value. They protect it.

Compliance Is Legitimacy, Not Bureaucracy

Every organization operates within rules: tax, employment, licensing, regulatory, and industry standards. Ignoring them does not create freedom; it creates exposure. The goal is not perfection but legitimacy:

- Operate lawfully in your industry and location
- Reduce preventable penalties and disruptions
- Remain credible with partners, investors, and customers
- Avoid costly "clean-up mode" during growth

Many founders wait until they are bigger to address compliance. Growth only amplifies existing risk.

Permits and Licenses: Invisible Until They Stop Everything

Permits and licenses rarely matter — until they suddenly do. *They determine what you are allowed to do, where you can operate, and which standards you must meet.* Even early-stage organizations should confirm required registrations, certifications, and reporting. Interruptions mid-momentum almost always cost more than early preparation.

Intellectual Property: Don't Build Value You Don't Own

Much of an organization's early value is intellectual property, including brand identity, frameworks and methods, content and training materials, software, designs, and proprietary systems. When ownership is unclear, disputes arise. When protection is weak, imitation follows. When documentation is missing, valuation suffers. Protection does not need to be complex — but it must be intentional.

Why This Matters for Scale and Exit

Investors, partners, and acquirers assess exposure as much as opportunity. Compliance gaps, missing permits, and unclear IP ownership delay deals, reduce valuation, weaken leverage, and increase perceived risk. Strong organizations do not eliminate risk. They manage it early — before it compounds.

Reflect & Practice

Reflection Prompts

- If you stepped away for 90 days, what would break first — vision clarity, decision-making, or execution discipline?
- Which parts of your organization still rely on assumptions, informal agreements, or your personal involvement rather than documented structure?
- What legal, regulatory, or intellectual property risks could quietly undermine everything you are building if left unaddressed?

Practice Challenge

For the next week:

1. Identify one source of fragility across vision, planning, structure, or protection.
2. Review one foundational document (VID, strategic plan, operating agreement, or compliance requirement) and note what is unclear, missing, or outdated.
3. Schedule one conversation with the right professional or advisor (strategic, legal, financial, or operational) to stress-test your assumptions.

Formation is not about perfection. It is about reducing preventable fragility.

With vision documented, authority clarified, plans disciplined, and protections in place, the organization stops relying on memory. *Chapter 5 moves from structure to people* — building the team, advisors, and early culture that will carry what you have formed forward.

Chapter 5
Build the Team, Advisors, & Early Culture

"If you want to go fast, go alone. If you want to go far, go together." **African Proverb**

Choose the right people. Shape early culture. Surround yourself with wisdom. Build together, not alone.

U p to this point, formation has focused on clarity, structure, and protection. Now the most unpredictable variable enters the picture: people. Ideas do not fail on their own. Documents do not drift on their own. Organizations derail when people are misaligned, miscast, or misled. This chapter is not about hiring quickly. It is about building human infrastructure that can carry vision, execute strategy, and sustain culture as the organization grows.

Early teams are small, informal, and high-trust. Roles overlap. Everyone does a bit of everything. That is exactly why early people decisions matter most. <u>In the early stage, every hire, advisor, or partner carries disproportionate leverage.</u> One person can:

- Accelerate momentum or derail it
- Stabilize execution or slow progress
- Reinforce values or quietly undermine them

Early teams do more than execute work. They define how work gets done. I have seen strong strategies stall because one early hire set the wrong tone — and modest ideas outperform expectations because early leaders were aligned, disciplined, and values-driven.

Culture is not something you add later. It is something you allow or design from the beginning.

Founders often treat team building, advisory support, and culture as separate conversations. In reality, they are deeply connected. *Your team executes the strategy. Your advisors shape decisions. Your culture governs behavior when no one is watching.* When these are misaligned, friction is inevitable. This chapter approaches people as a system — not a collection of individuals.

When early people decisions are rushed or reactive, the consequences compound:

- Founders become bottlenecks
- Accountability blurs
- Conflict becomes personal
- Performance issues linger
- Culture fragments under pressure

These problems rarely explode immediately. They erode trust quietly until growth exposes them. Fixing people problems later is far more expensive than designing for alignment early.

This chapter is not about building a large team. It is about building the right foundation of people. The organization will eventually outgrow you — but it will never outgrow the culture you allow.

We begin with the most sensitive question of all: ***who should be at the table, and in what role, from the beginning?***
That is where Section 5.1 begins.

5.1 Selecting Founders and Key Roles

Few decisions shape an organization more than who is involved at the beginning — and in what capacity. <u>Many founders choose early partners based on availability, loyalty, or shared frustration.</u>

Sometimes that works. More often, it creates ambiguity that surfaces later, when the stakes are higher and separation is costly. This section is not about discouraging partnership. It is about clarifying roles before emotion hardens into ownership.

Founder Is a Role — Not a Sentiment

Being a founder is not about belief alone. It is about responsibility, risk, and long-term accountability. A founder:

- Carries legal and financial exposure
- Shapes culture through behavior, not intention
- Influences decisions long after launch
- Remains accountable when things go wrong

Not everyone who supports the idea should be a founder. *Not everyone who works early should own equity.* Confusing contribution with ownership is one of the most common early mistakes.

Founders, Leaders, and Contributors

Healthy organizations distinguish clearly between:

- **Founders** – long-term direction, risk, and stewardship
- **Key leaders** – execution and decision authority
- **Contributors** – delivery without governance responsibility

When these distinctions blur, tension follows.

I have seen close friends start a company without addressing decision rights, growth, scale, or exit expectations. Early consensus masked differences. As success came, one wanted stability while the other wanted scale. The conflict became personal — and ended the company. Clarity would not have damaged the relationship. Ambiguity did.

Complementarity Beats Comfort

Founders often choose partners who think and work like them. That feels efficient early — and fragile later. Strong founding teams are complementary: vision balanced with execution, creativity with discipline, risk with restraint. ***Diversity of strength is an asset when roles are clear.*** Without clarity, it becomes conflict.

Roles Must Serve the Mission

Early roles are often shaped around people instead of purpose. Titles are given to reward loyalty or avoid hard conversations. Over time, those roles become constraints. I have seen investors walk away not because the business lacked potential, but because the founder's authority was unclear. *Capital follows clarity.* It avoids friction.

Why This Matters for Scale and Exit

Founder and role decisions affect governance, equity flexibility, investor confidence, succession, and exit negotiations. <u>Many exits fail not because value was missing, but because ownership and authority were contested.</u> Clarity early preserves options later.

Before formalizing any founder or key role, ask:

- What responsibility does this role carry?
- What authority does it require?
- What accountability comes with it?
- What happens if this person exits?

If those answers are uncomfortable, that discomfort is the signal.

Once founders and key roles are clear, the next step is deciding ***how people enter the organization*** — as employees, contractors, or partners — and under what expectations. That is where *Section 5.2 begins.*

5.2 Hiring, Contracting, and Staffing Early

How people enter matters more than how fast you grow. Once key roles are defined, the critical decision is not *who* to bring in — but *how* they enter the organization. Early founders often blur hiring, contracting, and partnering out of urgency. It works briefly. Then confusion sets in.

Employees, contractors, and partners are **not interchangeable.** Each carries different expectations around commitment, accountability, cost, flexibility, and control. Problems arise when founders expect:

- Employee loyalty from contractors
- Partner-level ownership from employees
- Contractor flexibility from partners

Clarity Upfront Prevents Friction Later

Early staffing decisions should follow strategy, not pressure. Not every need requires a full-time hire. Not every gap should be filled permanently. Speed sometimes matters — but flexibility often matters more.

Contracts are part of design, not distrust. Even simple agreements:

- Define scope and boundaries
- Clarify expectations
- Protect relationships when pressure increases

At this stage, the goal is not building a large team. It is assembling the **right mix of capability,** *at the* **right level of commitment,** for the organization's current phase. The patterns set here quietly shape how people are hired, managed, and trusted later.

Who You Let In Determines How Far You Can Go

In *Good to Great*, **Jim Collins** found that enduring organizations focused on *who before what*. Before strategy, growth, or execution, they ensured the right people were in the right seats — and misaligned ones exited early.

Talent alone is not enough. Skill without alignment creates drag. Competence without shared values introduces risk. One misaligned early hire can quietly undo momentum long before results decline.

When identity is clear, hiring becomes a filter instead of a guess. That is how organizations protect momentum before growth tests it.

Once people enter, something begins forming immediately — whether designed or not. That force is culture. That is where *Section 5.3* begins.

5.3. Designing Culture from Day One

Culture does not begin when the team grows. It begins the moment the first person joins. Many founders assume culture emerges later — once the organization is bigger or more formal. In reality, culture forms immediately through behavior, decisions, and what is tolerated or rewarded.

Before values are written, culture is already being lived. Early culture takes shape through:

- How decisions are made
- How conflict is handled
- How feedback is given
- How accountability is enforced
- How pressure is absorbed

Founders often underestimate how quickly these patterns solidify. As explored more deeply in dedicated work on organizational culture, culture forms long before it is named — and becomes difficult to undo once reinforced. Early on, three dynamics matter most:

1. What you excuse becomes precedent
2. What you reward becomes expectation
3. What you avoid becomes culture

Culture Is Formed Before It Is Named

This is why culture cannot be delegated or postponed. It must be designed intentionally — even when the team is small and informal. *Culture is not about perks or slogans.* It is about standards. It quietly answers questions like:

- How do we treat each other under pressure?
- What behaviors build trust — and which ones break it?
- What does "good work" actually mean here?
- What will not be tolerated, even if results are strong?

Early hires learn culture less from orientation and more from observation. What founders do matters more than what they say. A few people behaving consistently will set the tone for dozens later.

The goal at this stage is not perfection. It is coherence — alignment between stated intent and daily behavior. If culture is not designed early, it will still form. It just will not form in your favor.

In the next section, we turn to the people who help founders think beyond themselves — advisors who bring perspective, protection, and strategic restraint. That is where **Section 5.4** begins.

5.4. Building Your Advisory Circle (CPA, Attorney, Strategists)

No founder builds something lasting alone. Even strong founders eventually hit limits — not of effort, but of perspective. Blind spots form quietly. Decisions carry more weight. Risk compounds faster than experience alone can manage.

In *Organizing Genius*, **Warren Bennis** showed that enduring breakthroughs rarely come from lone visionaries. They emerge from "Great Groups" — small, diverse circles built around shared purpose, mutual respect, and the freedom to challenge one another. Scale does not require being the smartest person in the room. It requires creating rooms where thinking improves through productive tension. Advisors are not operators.

- They are not employees.
- They are not cheerleaders.
- They are stabilizers and accelerators.

An effective advisory circle helps founders slow down before costly mistakes, pressure-test decisions, and see consequences early — when options still exist.

Advisors Reduce Blind Spots

Founders live inside the organization. Advisors stand outside it. That distance matters. Good advisors help founders:

- Challenge assumptions before reality does
- Separate urgency from importance
- See risks emotional investment can hide
- Think several moves ahead
- Open doors when leverage is needed

Advisors exist to surface what founders cannot easily see from inside the work.

Be Intentional About Who You Invite

Advisors should not be chosen based on availability or proximity. They should be selected for perspective, restraint, and alignment. <u>Strong advisory relationships are framed as mutual exchanges, not favors.</u> This requires clarity on the advisor's role and value, alignment on expectations and boundaries, and defined scope, cadence, and simple MOU. Structure protects both sides and keeps advice focused on impact.

Core Advisors Most Founders Need Early

While advisory circles evolve, most founders benefit early from three perspectives:

1. **Legal Advisor (Attorney)** – structure, governance, contracts, and risk
2. **Financial Advisor (CPA or CFO-level)** – cash flow, tax, compliance, and economic reality
3. **Strategic Advisor (Operator or Industry Expert)** – positioning, tradeoffs, and scale logic

Advisors do not need to be full-time. They need to be trusted, honest, and aligned.

Alignment Matters More Than Credentials

The most dangerous advisors are not inexperienced ones — they are misaligned ones. Advisors must understand the mission, values, scale intent, and exit horizon. Without alignment, advice fragments. With alignment, decision quality improves.

No major decision should rely on a single perspective — especially your own.

Reflect & Practice

Reflection Questions

- Where am I currently making people decisions based on urgency rather than intention?
- Which roles or responsibilities am I still carrying that should not belong to me long-term?
- What kind of culture am I unintentionally modeling through my daily behavior?
- Who is influencing my decisions right now — and who should be?

Practice Challenge (7 Days)

Over the next week:

1. Identify one role, decision, or responsibility you should stop carrying alone.
2. List three qualities your early team or advisors must embody — beyond skills.
3. Write one sentence describing the culture you want others to experience before it is ever named.

Culture is not declared. It is demonstrated — and reinforced by the people you choose.

Up to this point, we have focused on people because organizations are built by humans before they are run by systems. In **Chapter 6**, we move from people to execution — forming the organization legally and operationally so it can transact, operate, and prepare for launch with discipline. This is where vision moves from conversation to structure.

Chapter 6
Form the Organization Legally & Operationally

"Without systems, even the best intentions collapse under pressure." **Gary Keller**, Founder of Keller Williams Real Estate Brokerage

Register properly. Set up systems. Establish operations. Create order that supports momentum.

By now, the organization exists in clarity — purpose has been defined, people have been identified, foundational, and legal documents are in place. What does not yet exist is *operational reality.* This chapter marks a critical transition:

• From planning to presence,
• From vision to execution, and
• From idea to institution.

Many founders underestimate this phase. They assume formation is paperwork — a checklist to complete before *"real work"* begins. In reality, this is where credibility is established, risk is contained, and momentum becomes possible. An organization that is not formed properly:

• Struggles to transact
• Creates confusion for partners and clients
• Raises red flags for investors
• Accumulates legal and financial risk silently

Formation is not about bureaucracy. It is about legitimacy. And that is why this chapter exists. It helps you form your organization in a way that supports growth, protects value, and prepares you for launch.

6.1 Registering the Entity and Tax Setup

There is a moment when an idea becomes real. <u>Once the entity is registered and the tax structure is set, the organization exists legally, financially, and operationally.</u> This step may feel procedural, but it is strategic — because early structural choices shape what becomes possible later.

Entity Formation Is a Strategic Choice

Many founders rush registration just to get started. The risk is not speed, but *unconscious choice*. Entity structure quietly affects:

- Liability exposure
- Tax efficiency
- Investor participation
- Ownership transitions
- Exit options

What works in year one can constrain options by year five.

Treat the Organization as an Entity

Garrett Sutton warns that many founders form entities on paper but operate as if nothing changed — mixing finances, skipping documentation, and ignoring governance. When this happens, courts, banks, and investors respond the same way. Treating the company as a real entity is not bureaucracy. It is the first signal that it is designed to outlast the founder.

Structure Misalignment Kills Deals

I once worked with a founder who built a profitable business and attracted investor interest — until the entity structure surfaced. Equity participation was complex, tax consequences were severe, and the deal stalled. Nothing was broken. The structure simply did not match the trajectory. You see this often on *Shark Tank*: interest disappears once entity misalignment shows up.

Tax Setup Shapes Behavior

Tax structure is not just an accounting issue. It shapes how founders operate. When tax implications are unclear:

- Cash feels unpredictable
- Decisions slow down
- Growth creates anxiety

Thoughtful tax setup influences pricing, hiring, reinvestment, and long-term wealth. It should be designed with experienced guidance.

Separation Protects the Organization

Proper registration and tax setup separate personal risk from organizational risk, individual finances from business cash flow, and short-term survival from long-term strategy. That separation allows the organization to grow beyond the founder's nervous system.

Early decisions rarely fail immediately. They echo later — when capital is raised, partners are added, or exit conversations begin. Formation is not about compliance alone. It is about preserving optionality.

With the legal foundation in place, the next step is ensuring money flows cleanly and transparently through the organization. That is where financial systems begin — and where **Section 6.2** takes us next.

6.2 Opening Bank Accounts & Financial Systems

Once the entity is formed, money begins to move — and this is where many founders blur boundaries. Personal accounts are used *"temporarily."* Spreadsheets replace systems. Performance is judged by bank balance or gut feel. Early on, this feels manageable. Later, it becomes expensive.

Financial Systems Create Clarity

Financial systems are not about sophistication. They are about separation, visibility, and trust. I have seen founders with strong revenue struggle to explain their numbers to investors, and others avoid growth opportunities simply because their financial picture was unclear.

One founder I worked with ran a profitable healthcare company, but all transactions flowed through a single account — taxes, payroll, vendors, and personal expenses mixed together. When an investor asked for basic financials, the conversation stalled. Not because the business was weak, but because the story could not be proven. That delay cost over a year of growth.

Separation Builds Credibility

Dedicated business accounts and basic financial systems allow founders to:

- See patterns instead of guessing
- Build trust with investors, partners, and lenders
- Protect the organization legally and operationally
- Reduce stress caused by financial ambiguity

You do not need perfection. You need discipline.

The Cost of Waiting

Many founders delay systems because revenue feels *"too small."* Ironically, those are the organizations that struggle most when revenue grows. Without clarity, growth creates anxiety instead of confidence. Financial clarity does not restrict creativity. It funds it.

Financial systems also send a signal: this organization is real, managed, and trustworthy.

Execution Turns Design Into Results

Andy Grove argued in *High Output Management* that success is determined not by ideas or strategy, but by execution — systems, routines, and disciplined follow-through. Legal formation gives permission to operate. Operational discipline determines whether the organization performs.

When execution is left to improvisation, scale becomes fragile, and founder dependence increases. Financial systems are among the first tests of whether design is becoming reality.

With financial foundations in place, the next step is building the operational tools that allow the organization to function consistently — even without the founder present. That is where we go next.

6.3. Tools, Systems, Platforms (CRM, website, ops, finance)

At this stage, speed increases and memory starts to fail. Conversations multiply. ***Information scatters across emails, notes, spreadsheets, and people's heads.*** What once worked through hustle becomes fragile. This is where systems stop being optional.

Systems are not about sophistication. They are about relief.

Systems Replace Memory

Early on, founders carry everything — decisions, follow-ups, client details, and context. That works briefly. But memory does not scale. Organizations built on memory eventually slow, stall, or fracture. Systems exist to offload cognitive burden so work can continue without constant founder involvement.

I once worked with a founder who said, "I took one week off and everything stalled." Nothing broke technically. Everything simply depended on her. *The problem was not leadership. It was the absence of systems.*

Working *In* vs Building *The* Business

Michael Gerber explains why many growing businesses stall: founders build operations that depend on their presence instead of systems that operate independently. The result is predictable — the founder becomes the *bottleneck*, **decisions pile up, and scale creates stress instead of leverage.**

If the business cannot run without you, you do not own a business. You own a job.

Tools Support Strategy; They Do Not Create It

Founders often chase tools hoping they will fix deeper problems. But tools only amplify what already exists:

- Clear processes become efficient
- Messy processes become faster messes

The goal is not more tools. It is clarity supported by systems.

Core Systems to Establish Early

You do not need everything. You do need the basics working together:

- **CRM** to track leads, clients, and communication
- **Public platforms** (website, landing pages, social channels) to clearly communicate value
- **Operational systems** to manage delivery, funnels, automation, workflows
- **Financial systems** to track revenue, expenses, and cash flow

Together, these form the organization's nervous system.

Reliability Creates Opportunity

One small organization I worked with had modest revenue but clean systems. When a larger partner conducted diligence, data was organized, and processes were visible. They did not look scrappy. They looked stable — and that perception created opportunity.

Start simple. Design for growth. <u>The mistake is not starting small. It is starting sloppily.</u>

With systems in place, the final step of formation is not building more. It is preparing wisely for launch without unnecessary exposure. That is where **Section 6.4** takes us next.

6.4. Preparing for Launch Readiness

At this stage, founders often feel pressure to move. The entity is formed. Accounts are open. Systems exist. The instinct is to announce and push forward. ***But launch is not a moment. It is a condition.***

Launch Is Readiness, Not Visibility

Founders often equate launch with publicity. True readiness asks a harder question: *If demand increases tomorrow, will the organization hold?*

I once worked with a founder whose launch exceeded expectations — leads surged, then response times slipped, delivery lagged, and trust eroded. The problem was not demand. It was preparedness.

What Readiness Actually Means

Before going public, founders should be able to answer:

- Can we deliver consistently?
- Are decision rights clear?
- Do systems hold under pressure?
- Can issues be resolved without escalation?

If the answer is unclear, visibility will amplify strain instead of progress.

Effectiveness Before Activity

Peter Drucker warned that effectiveness precedes efficiency. Busyness creates motion, not progress. At launch, the discipline is focus before force. Fewer right actions outperform many unfocused ones. Readiness is precision — not speed.

Test Before You Expose

Well-designed organizations validate internally before going public. Pilots, limited rollouts, or quiet trials prove delivery, decision flow, and system resilience. <u>A soft launch is not caution. It is maturity.</u>

Readiness Builds Confidence

When an organization is ready:

- Teams act with clarity
- Customers feel stability
- Partners trust execution

That confidence compounds.

Launching does not end the work. It shifts it — from internal preparation to controlled exposure and learning.

Reflect & Practice
Reflection Prompts

- Where does my organization still depend on me personally instead of structure, systems, or clear rules?
- Which assumptions about taxes, cash flow, or compliance could create pressure once activity increases?
- If we launched publicly tomorrow, what part of the organization would be exposed first — financially, operationally, or structurally?

Practice Challenge (7 Days)

1. Identify one structural or financial decision that needs to be documented rather than held in your head.
2. Stress-test one system (cash flow, approvals, reporting, delivery) under a realistic growth scenario.
3. Clarify one decision boundary that currently depends on you and assign it to a role or rule.

Formation is not about perfection. It is about readiness. You have now completed the work of *formation* — turning vision into legal reality, plans into systems, and intent into operating discipline.

In **Part III**, we move from building the organization to introducing it to the world — launching with control, learning without chaos, and stabilizing before scale.

That is where execution begins.

PART III

LAUNCH & STABILIZE

"Vision without execution is hallucination. Execution without refinement is chaos." **Thomas Edison**, Inventor and Entrepreneur

Test boldly. Launch thoughtfully. Refine repeatedly. Strengthen what holds everything together.

Design gives clarity. Formation gives structure. Launch is where reality responds. This is where ideas meet customers, systems meet pressure, and assumptions meet evidence. *Launch is not a single event. It is a phase,* and how founders move through it determines whether momentum becomes stability or collapse.

Most organizations do not fail at launch because they lack determination. They fail because they confuse speed with readiness:

- They rush to market without testing
- They scale messaging before delivery is consistent
- They chase visibility before trust is built

<u>Launch exposes what design and formation either prepared for — or ignored.</u>

Launch Is a Discipline, Not a Moment

Launch is not about being seen. It is about being proven. This phase demands learning quickly, adjusting decisively, and resisting the urge to overpromise before systems can deliver. *The goal is not explosive growth. It is controlled learning.*

In this stage:

- Every customer interaction is feedback
- Every delivery tests repeatability
- Every delay reveals a bottleneck

Founders who treat launch as experimentation gain leverage. Those who treat it as performance inherit fragility.

The Risk of Premature Scale

A common mistake is scaling attention faster than capability. Demand increases, delivery cracks, quality slips, and founders step back into operations to compensate. That is not growth. It is debt.

Launch should strengthen the organization, not strain it. That requires <u>testing before committing, learning before amplifying, and refining before expanding.</u>

Where Culture and Systems Are Tested

Culture does not form in planning sessions. It forms under pressure. Launch reveals how decisions are made, whether values hold, and whether systems support execution or rely on founder. *What is tolerated here becomes normalized later.*

What Part III Focuses On

Part III helps you move from formation to traction without losing control. You will learn how to:

- Launch in phases instead of betting on a single moment
- Deliver consistently while improving continuously
- Identify and fix bottlenecks early
- Stabilize operations before scaling demand

This is where discipline replaces adrenaline.

From Formation to Traction

In Part II, you formed the organization legally, operationally, and culturally. In Part III, you put that formation under real-world conditions, strengthen what holds, and turn early wins into repeatable performance.

Launch is not about proving you are ready. It is about becoming ready.

That work begins in **Chapter 7** — by launching strategically, not recklessly.

Chapter 7
Launch Strategically — Soft, Official, & Ongoing

"The greatest danger in launching anything is launching too late." **Reid Hoffman**, Founder of LinkedIn

Pilot thoughtfully. Launch boldly. Communicate clearly. Treat launch as a phase, not a moment.

L aunch is where reality begins. Up to this point, much of the work has been internal. You clarified purpose. You designed identity. You chose structure. You formed the organization. Now something shifts. If Chapter 6 was about proving readiness internally, this chapter is about testing reality externally — without gambling trust, capital, or credibility. At this stage, the organization leaves your head and enters the world.

This is where many founders feel both excitement and anxiety — and for good reason. <u>Launch is the first moment your assumptions are tested by people who did not help you build the idea.</u>

Customers do not care how great your vision, design, or how hard you worked. Markets do not reward intention. Reality responds only to what actually functions.

I've seen founders spend months perfecting plans, only to freeze at launch. I've seen others rush to market too quickly, believing momentum will fix everything later. Both approaches are costly.

Launch is not about speed. It is about *sequence*.

This chapter is about launching in a way that protects learning, preserves trust, and builds momentum without forcing scale too early.

Launch Is a Phase, Not an Event

One of the most damaging myths in entrepreneurship is the idea that launch is a single moment — a date on the calendar. In reality, launch happens in phases:

- You test quietly.
- You go public intentionally.
- You refine continuously.

Founders who treat launch as a moment tend to panic when things wobble. Founders who treat launch as a process stay grounded when adjustments are required.

This chapter walks through that process — beginning with the soft launch.

7.1. Soft Launch (testing, prototyping, pilots)

A soft launch is where you learn without paying full price for mistakes. It is not about playing small. It is about playing smart.

What a Soft Launch Really Does

A soft launch lets you observe how the organization behaves under real, limited pressure. Not hypotheticals — real customers. This is where you discover:

- What people misunderstand
- Where friction exists
- Which assumptions were wrong
- Where the founder is still the bottleneck

The goal is not applause. It is evidence.

Learning Before You Scale Exposure

Eric Ries emphasized validated learning — testing assumptions through rapid experimentation before scaling exposure. Founders who skip this step often confuse activity with progress. They launch loudly, invest heavily, and only later discover confusion, misalignment, or weak demand.

Lean founders ask early:

- What must be true for this to work?
- What can we test quickly and cheaply?
- What feedback would force a change?

Constraint Builds Scalable Strength

In *Start-Up Nation*, Dan Senor and Saul Singer showed that organizations operating under constraint often scale better than those born in comfort. Limited resources force clarity, ownership, and decisive execution. Those muscles, built early, carry forward.

Soft launches create those learning loops:

1. They protect capital
2. They protect morale
3. They protect credibility

Scaling amplifies what already exists. A soft launch ensures what exists is worth amplifying.

I once worked with a founder convinced that pricing was the issue. A soft launch revealed the real problem: onboarding. Customers didn't know what success looked like. Clarifying onboarding increased conversions without changing price — a lesson that would have been costly to learn publicly.

Forms a Soft Launch Can Take

A soft launch does not need to be formal. It might be:

- A pilot with a small cohort
- A beta with early adopters
- A limited release to one segment
- A service delivered manually before systematization

The intent is clarity, not polish.

What to Watch Closely

During a soft launch, observe:

- Where customers hesitate
- Where explanations are required
- Where delivery depends on you
- Where systems lag under light demand

Soft launches reveal fragility while it is still fixable. That is their power.

7.2. Official Launch (events, PR, campaigns)

An official launch is when you *turn the volume up*. But volume only helps if the signal is clear.

The Purpose of an Official Launch

The official launch is not validation. Validation already happened quietly during soft launch. The official launch is ***amplification***. This is where you:

- Increase visibility
- Expand outreach
- Invite broader attention
- Begin operating at a higher cadence

I've seen founders confuse this and try to validate in public. When things break, they feel exposed — not because failure occurred, but because learning was rushed. <u>Learning belongs in the soft launch.</u> <u>Visibility belongs here.</u>

Signals You Are Ready for an Official Launch

You do not need perfection. You do need stability. Ask yourself:

- Can customers understand the offer without explanation?
- Can the team deliver without improvisation?
- Can issues be resolved without founder intervention every time?

If the answer is mostly yes, you are ready. If not, delay visibility — not out of fear, but out of discipline.

7.3. Customer Onboarding and Early Delivery Models

Early customers shape your future more than later ones. They become:

- Your First Testimonials
- Your First Critics
- Your First Raving Fans
- Your First Referrals — Or Warnings

How you onboard and deliver early does more than satisfy customers. It trains your organization how to serve.

Onboarding Is the First Test of Trust

Onboarding is not administrative. It is emotional. It answers unspoken questions:

- Am I in the right place?
- Do these people know what they are doing?
- What does success look like here?

I've watched strong offers fail because onboarding felt chaotic. Customers assumed the chaos reflected deeper problems — even when the core service was solid.

Clarity builds confidence. Confusion creates doubt.

Early Delivery Sets the Pattern

What you repeat in the early days becomes your default — and eventually, your culture. If early delivery:

- Requires daring
- Depends on the founder's presence
- Changes every time

Scale will not fix it. Scale will amplify exhaustion.

Early delivery should be simple, repeatable, and explainable — even if imperfect. This is where founders begin transitioning from doing the work *to* designing how the work gets done.

Support Is the First Signal of Trustworthiness

No onboarding or delivery process is perfect. Things break down. Instructions misread. Systems crumble. Expectations drift.

What separates durable organizations from fragile ones is not whether problems occur — but how they are handled when they do.

Early customers are watching closely:

- Is there a clear path to support?
- Are issues acknowledged quickly?
- Is responsibility taken, or deflected?
- Does a human step in when automation fails?

I've experienced this on both sides — as a customer and as a consultant. <u>When support is responsive and composed, trust deepens even after a mistake. When support is slow, confusing, or defensive, confidence erodes fast.</u>

Support is not an add-on to delivery. It *is* delivery — especially in the early stage.

Organizations that design basic support early — clear contact points, simple escalation rules, and human backup when systems fail — recover faster, learn quicker, and retain trust longer.

Design for Learning, Not Perfection

Early onboarding, delivery, and support are not about getting everything right. They are about seeing clearly. Each interaction reveals:

- Where customers hesitate
- Where expectations are unclear
- Where systems lag behind demand
- Where the founder is still the bottleneck

Founders who pay attention here design better models. Those who rush past this phase hard-code fragility into the organization.

This chapter is not about operational excellence or performance optimization. Those disciplines come next in **Chapter 8**. Here, the focus is narrower and more human: *what customers experience when they first say yes.*

Early delivery is not about proving excellence. It is about establishing trust. Excellence is designed later — after reliability is proven and trust is earned. And *reliability and trust are what scale.*

7.4. Momentum Building Strategies (message, media, outreach)

Momentum is not created by intensity. It is created by consistency.

How Momentum Actually Builds

Momentum comes from:

- A message repeated clearly
- A delivery experience people talk about
- A presence that feels steady, not frantic

I've seen founders burn out chasing every channel:

1. LinkedIn today.
2. YouTube tomorrow.
3. TikTok next week.
4. A webinar next month.

Nothing compounds. The founders who win choose fewer channels and show up with discipline. <u>Momentum is not acceleration. Momentum is rhythm.</u> And rhythm allows you to grow without losing control.

Growth Requires Response, Not Activity

Dan Kennedy has long warned that growth fails not because organizations lack effort, but because they lack response. In his work on direct response and business discipline, he makes a simple but uncomfortable point: *activity does not equal progress.*

Marketing that generates attention without measurable response creates motion without leverage. <u>Scale, in contrast, requires that every message, offer, and outreach effort produce signal — something that can be tested, tracked, and improved.</u>

This discipline matters early. Organizations that build momentum without response confuse noise for traction and volume for validation. Sustainable growth demands feedback from the market, not applause from it.

Reflect & Practice
Reflection Prompts

- Which parts of your launch should be tested quietly before being amplified?
- Where are you still relying on yourself instead of systems?
- What signals would tell you that you are ready for broader visibility?

Practice Challenge (7 Days)

Over the next week:

- Identify one assumption you are making about customers, delivery, support, visibility, or messaging.
- Test it with a small group.
- Adjust one element of your launch based on what you learn.

Learning early is cheaper than repairing later.

Launching gets you into the market. Staying there requires discipline. In the next chapter, we move from launch activity to operational excellence — delivering consistently, measuring performance, and preventing early momentum from turning into early chaos. That is where stability begins.

Chapter 8
Deliver, Improve, & Build Early Operational Excellence

"Excellence is never an accident. It is always the result of high intention, sincere effort, and intelligent execution." **Aristotle,** Greek Philosopher and Polymath

Deliver well. Listen closely. Refine continuously. Build excellence into every process.

L aunching gets attention. Delivery determines credibility. This is where organizations stop being ideas and start becoming realities. Promises are tested, expectations harden, and trust is earned or lost through execution.

I have seen founders with strong brands and compelling launches lose momentum here — not because the market rejected them, but because delivery exposed gaps they did not know existed. Early operational excellence is not about perfection. It is about reliability under pressure.

Many organizations do not fail loudly at this stage. They lose credibility quietly — one missed expectation, one inconsistent delivery, one overwhelmed founder at a time.

Why Delivery Is a Leadership Issue

Founders often treat delivery as an operational problem to solve later — after hiring, systems, or funding. That mindset is backward. Delivery is a leadership issue first.

Early delivery signals:

- What standards matter
- What "good enough" means
- How problems are handled
- Whether commitments are firm or flexible

Teams learn from what is tolerated far more than from what is stated. *If excellence is optional early, it becomes negotiable later.* Discipline must begin while things are still small.

The Hidden Cost of Early Chaos

Early chaos often feels normal — everyone busy, improvising, doing their best. But chaos has a cost.

Unchecked, it leads to:

- Founder bottlenecks
- Emotional decision-making
- Burnout disguised as commitment
- Customer confusion framed as "growth pains"

The goal is not to eliminate friction. It is to prevent *avoidable friction* from becoming culture.

Excellence Is Designed, Not Discovered

Operational excellence is intentional. It is built through:

- Clear delivery standards
- Simple visibility into performance
- Repeatable processes
- Feedback loops that improve without panic

This does not require heavy systems or bureaucracy. <u>Over-engineering early can be as damaging as neglect.</u> What matters is deciding what must be done consistently, by whom, and how success is measured.

What This Chapter Will Help You Build

This chapter focuses on four early disciplines:

- Delivering in ways that set sustainable standards
- Measuring what matters before emotions take over
- Reducing founder dependence through simple systems
- Improving continuously without destabilizing the organization

You are not building for volume yet. *You are building for repeatability.* That is what allows excellence to survive growth.

8.1. Delivering and Overdelivering (initial customer success)

Early delivery is not about impressing customers. It is about earning trust under real conditions.

At launch, everything is amplified. Promises feel louder. Delays feel longer. Mistakes feel personal. Customers are not just evaluating what you deliver. **They are watching** how *you deliver it*: responsiveness, predictability, and how you respond when things break.

Your first customers are not only buying a product or service. <u>They are buying confidence in your organization.</u>

When Enthusiasm Outruns Readiness

This pattern is common. Launch demand exceeds expectations. The numbers look great — but the delivery cycle was never fully tested. What follows is predictable:

- Onboarding lags

- Timelines slip
- Support requests pile up
- Manual work replaces systems
- The founder steps in to "save it"

The issue is rarely effort. It is untested delivery.

The harder question founders must ask early is simple: *What happens operationally if demand doubles tomorrow?* Early customer success depends on whether delivery has been pressure-tested end to end — fulfillment, communication, billing, follow-up, and support.

Overdelivering Is About Focus, Not Excess

Overdelivering does not mean doing everything for everyone. That leads to burnout and inconsistency. Intentional overdelivery means being generous where it matters most to customer success — and disciplined everywhere else.

A grounding question helps: ***What does success look like for the customer in their first 30–60 days?*** Founders who answer this design delivery around outcomes, not activity. Those who don't default to effort instead of intention.

Early delivery sets expectations. And expectations become standards.

Delivery Breaks Reveal Leadership Gaps

Things will break. Delays will happen. Instructions will be misunderstood. <u>None of that is fatal. How founders respond is what determines trust.</u>

Early customers notice:

- How quickly issues are acknowledged
- Whether responsibility is taken or deflected

- Whether systems handle problems or everything depends on the founder

Support is not separate from delivery. It is delivery in the early stage.

Founders who design basic safeguards early — simple automation, human backup, and clear escalation paths — recover faster, retain trust longer, and learn more quickly.

Test Before You Scale Attention

Early delivery is not about proving excellence. It is about discovering fragility before it becomes public.

Founders who test the full delivery cycle — including failures and edge cases — build confidence that survives growth. Those who rely on enthusiasm alone often learn in public.

Early customer success is not about perfection. It is about reliability under pressure. And reliability is what scales.

8.2. Performance Dashboards & KPIs

Most founders do not struggle because they lack effort. They struggle because they lack visibility.

Pressure appears before patterns are understood. Revenue feels tight. Customers feel quieter. Teams feel stretched. Decisions become reactive. By the time emotion enters the room, the signal has usually been present for weeks — unnoticed. That is the cost of operating without performance visibility.

The Risk of Measuring the Wrong Things

Organizations often measure what is easiest to count instead of what sustains performance. Robert Kaplan and David Norton addressed this imbalance through the **Balanced Scorecard**, arguing that long-term results depend on balance across four dimensions:

- Financial results
- Customer experience
- Internal processes
- Learning and growth

When one dominates, organizations drift. Founders usually feel this imbalance before they can explain it. *Measurement exists to surface reality early* — before pressure forces decisions.

KPIs and OKRs Serve Different Purposes

KPIs and OKRs are two of the most widely used performance measurement frameworks worldwide. While they are closely related, they serve different purposes and are not interchangeable.

1. **KPIs** track business health. They answer: *How are we doing right now?* Examples include cash runway, conversion rates, delivery cycle time, retention, and capacity utilization.

2. **OKRs** drive focused improvement. They answer: *What must improve next?* Objectives set direction. Key Results define progress.

Used together:

- KPIs stabilize execution
- OKRs accelerate change

KPIs tell you where you are. OKRs help you move deliberately from there.

Metrics Create Candor Before Crisis

Jack Welch believed candor was a competitive advantage — and metrics made candor unavoidable. <u>Leaders were expected to know their numbers, explain drivers, and confront reality early.</u>

Scale does not break organizations because leaders lack vision. It breaks them because leaders tolerate ambiguity. Clear metrics replace ambiguity with clarity — and clarity enables decisive action.

Early Metrics Are About Learning, Not Impressing

Early-stage data will never be perfect. Waiting for perfection delays learning. Directionally honest indicators are enough:

- Track delivery time manually
- Measure response lag
- Count onboarding friction points
- Set simple weekly or monthly targets

Measurement is not about sophistication. It is about consistency.

I once worked with a founder convinced marketing was the problem. Three months of basic data showed the real issue was delivery delay. The dashboard did not just correct strategy — it corrected the story the founder was telling themselves.

Good Metrics Reduce Drama

Strong dashboards:

1. Calm decisions
2. Improve conversations
3. Shift energy from blame to improvement

When performance is visible, growth becomes understandable instead of chaotic.

Performance dashboards are not about control. They are about truth. And truth, faced early, is one of the strongest advantages a founder can build.

8.3. Systems That Prevent Chaos (founder bottlenecks)

Growth often slows not because people lack capability, but because too much depends on one person. Decisions pile up. Questions flow upward. The founder works harder — yet progress stalls. This is neither a motivation issue nor a capability gap. It is a systems problem.

Founders rarely choose to become bottlenecks. It happens quietly:

- They approve everything
- They answer every question
- They fix every problem

<u>Early on, this creates speed. As volume increases, it creates delay, dependency, and hesitation.</u> Teams wait instead of deciding. Growth exposes dependence instead of leverage.

The Shift That Unlocks Scale

Scaling requires an identity shift: Not How do I do this better? *But* how do I design this so it works without me?

That shift forces clarity around ownership. At a minimum, *growing organizations need clear ownership* — full-time, fractional, or interim — across core functions such as finance, delivery, systems, people, and customer experience. You do not need them fully staffed early. You do need them clearly owned.

Systems First, Processes Second

Systems organize responsibility. Processes organize execution.

Without systems, founders improvise. Without processes, teams guess. *Even simple structure reduces escalation and restores momentum.*

I once worked with a founder who thought motivation was the issue. The team was capable but overwhelmed. Everything still flowed through the founder. We clarified a handful of core systems, assigned ownership, and documented only the critical processes. Within weeks, decisions stopped escalating and delivery stabilized. Growth no longer required fortitude — only coordination.

Why Systems Hold Under Pressure

Research across disciplines points to the same conclusion:

- **Atul Gawande** showed that simple systems protect execution under overload.
- **Michael Gerber** warned that businesses fail when they depend on the founder instead of systems.
- **Andrew Grove** argued that leadership leverage comes from designing systems others can run.

Excellence is not achieved by doing more. It comes from consistently applying the fundamentals and not letting them slip.

From Heroics to Resilience

When systems replace ad hoc fixes:

- Decisions move faster
- Accountability becomes clearer
- Delivery becomes predictable
- Founders regain thinking space

Operational excellence is not perfection. It is predictability under pressure. The earlier systems are designed, the less chaos growth creates — and the more freedom scale provides.

This is where organizations stop surviving on effort and start operating on design.

8.4. Feedback Loops and Continuous Improvement

Early-stage organizations rarely fail because they make mistakes. They fail because they repeat the same mistakes without noticing.

At this stage, assumptions are being tested in real time. Customers are encountering your work for the first time. Systems are under pressure before they are stable. <u>Without feedback loops, delivery becomes guesswork and small issues quietly harden into habits.</u>

Feedback is how an organization learns faster than its environment changes. Without it, growth creates blind spots instead of insight.

From Fixing Problems to System-Level Thinking

Many teams practice single-loop learning: something breaks, it gets fixed, and work continues. The symptom disappears, but the underlying assumption remains.

Double-loop learning goes deeper. It asks not only *How do we fix this?* but *Why did this happen at all?*

The difference is decisive:

- Single-loop teams get better at firefighting
- Double-loop teams develop system-level thinking

Over time, system-level thinking — not quick fixes — determines organizational maturity and effectiveness.

Catching Strategic Inflection Points Early

Andrew Grove described *strategic inflection points* as moments when the fundamental assumptions behind a business begin to change.

What worked before starts to lose effectiveness, and continuing on the same path becomes increasingly dangerous.

These moments rarely announce themselves dramatically. They often appear quietly as recurring friction, slowing execution, unexpected customer reactions, emerging competitors, or feedback that feels uncomfortable to hear.

Feedback loops exist to surface these signals early—while adjustment is still manageable and learning is still fast. When ignored, the same signals do not disappear. They compound. What could have been a course correction later shows up as a crisis.

Organizations do not fail because inflection points occur. They fail because they recognize them too late—or refuse to question the assumptions that no longer hold.

Simple Loops That Work

Effective feedback does not require sophistication. It requires discipline. Early-stage loops should be short, frequent, and actionable:

- Brief customer check-ins after delivery
- Short internal debriefs after milestones
- Regular review of breakdowns and delays
- Clear ownership for acting on what is learned

The goal is not perfection. It is pattern recognition.

Feedback as a Cultural Signal

W. Edwards Deming showed that improvement is not an event. It is a system of learning. That system depends on safety. When leaders ask for feedback and respond without defensiveness, learning accelerates.

Feedback culture is not about being soft. It is about staying visible to reality.

When Success Becomes the Risk

Clayton Christensen warned that success itself can blind organizations. What worked before gets protected. Signals that challenge the model get filtered out.

Strong organizations ask two questions:

- How do we do this better?
- And: What if what made us successful is no longer enough?

Reflect & Practice
Reflection Prompts

1. Where does delivery feel inconsistent or overly dependent on you right now?
2. What signals are you sensing emotionally that may already exist in the data?
3. How does your organization currently respond to feedback — defensively, selectively, or deliberately?

Practice Challenge (7 Days)

- Identify one core delivery process and write it down as it actually happens.
- Define 3–5 simple indicators that tell you whether delivery is improving or slipping.
- Hold one short debrief (15 minutes max) focused only on learning, not fixing.

Operational excellence does not require complexity — only attention.

When delivery becomes predictable, improvement becomes intentional. And that stability is what allows momentum to turn into profit and scale.

Chapter 9
Stabilize, Make It Profitable, & Prepare for Scale

"Scaling amplifies whatever exists. If the foundation is weak, growth will expose it." **Ben Horowitz**, Author, Investor, and Businessman

Strengthen the core. Fix weaknesses. Achieve profitability. Build readiness before expansion.

There is a phase where growth looks like success — but stability has not caught up. Customers are coming in. Activity is high. From the outside, things look promising. Inside, pressure is quietly building. Margins feel thin. Cash moves fast. Founders remain involved in everything.

The organization is moving — but not grounded.

Chapter 8 focused on delivering well and building systems that survive pressure. Chapter 9 exists because execution alone is not enough. This is where organizations either stabilize — or slowly destabilize while appearing to grow.

Growth Is Not the Goal — Stability Is

Most founders are trained to chase growth. Growth without stability isn't scale. It's speed without control—and eventually, collapse.

I've seen founders with double revenue and still live in constant anxiety — stressed about payroll and unable to step away. I've also seen slower-growing organizations operate with confidence because their fundamentals were solid. The difference was not motivation. It was stabilization.

Stability turns effort into enterprise value. Profitability turns vision into longevity. Preparation turns growth into scale.

Why Smart Capital Avoids Unstable Growth

Experienced investors look beyond momentum. They look for discipline — predictable delivery, controlled decision-making, reliable cash flow, and leadership not operating in survival mode.

Rapid growth without stability signals risk, not opportunity. This is why stressed companies often attract opportunistic buyers. These buyers are not betting on growth. <u>They are buying dysfunction at a discount, installing discipline, and scaling later at valuations the founder never reached.</u>

Founders try to scale their way out of instability. *Savvy operators stabilize first* — then scale deliberately.

The "We'll Fix It Later" Trap

At this stage, founders delay hard decisions:

- "Margins will improve with volume."
- "We'll clean this up after the next push."
- "Let's not slow things down now."

So inefficiencies linger. Stress becomes normal. Chaos gets tolerated.

The longer instability persists, the more expensive it becomes to fix. Stability is not earned later. It is built into growth while the organization is still manageable.

Profitability Is a Discipline

Profitability is not a milestone. It is a way of operating —
understanding how money actually moves through pricing, costs,
delivery, and tradeoffs.

Revenue alone does not equal health. Profitability is not about greed.
It is about sustainability. Without it, scale is fragile. With it, growth
becomes optional — not desperate.

From Builder to Steward

This chapter marks a shift:

1. From builder to steward
2. From operator to system designer
3. From effort-driven growth to stability-driven scale

<u>Investors, teams, and partners are not asking whether you can grow.</u>
<u>They are asking whether your organization can hold what it grows.</u>

The organizations that last are not the ones that grow the fastest.
They are the ones that stabilize before they scale.

9.1. Path to Profitability (unit economics, cash flow basics)

Profitability is not optimism or momentum. It is math, and discipline.

I've worked with founders doing seven figures in revenue who still
lived in anxiety: payroll pressure, vendor stress, and personal savings
quietly propping up the business. Revenue gave confidence.
Profitability would have given control.

Unit Economics: Why One Sale Matters

In startup thinking, leaders are often encouraged to understand performance at the *unit level* before looking at totals. That unit may be:

- One client
- One product
- One contract

The fundamental question is simple: ***When we deliver this once, do we actually make money?***

If the answer is no, scaling only multiplies the problem.

Many founders avoid this because the answers are uncomfortable. I've seen businesses where flagship offers lost money, custom work exhausted teams, and discounts drove volume while profit disappeared. When unit economics don't work, growth scales effort — not value.

Profitability starts when each unit works on its own, before volume enters the picture.

Cash Flow Is the Scoreboard

You can be profitable on paper and still fail. Cash flow answers a different question: *Do you have money when you need it?*

Clients pay late. Expenses arrive early. Growth increases cash demand before it relieves pressure. I once worked with a company that doubled revenue in six months — and nearly missed payroll twice. Demand wasn't the problem. Cash flow design was.

At this stage, cash flow matters more than revenue.

Profitability Is a Design Choice

Profit is not earned later. It is designed into:

- Pricing decisions
- What you say yes to — and what you decline
- How standardized delivery is
- How dependent outcomes are on the founder

Scaling does not fix weak economics. It amplifies them.

Pricing Is Leverage, Not Risk

Many founders underprice long after credibility is earned. They fear friction, churn, or slowing momentum. In reality, *pricing is often the fastest path to stability.*

Well-justified price increases frequently improve margins immediately — without adding complexity. Strong margins are not greed. They are stewardship. They create room to stabilize, invest, and scale deliberately.

From Survival to Stewardship

Profitability allows you to:

- Step back without panic
- Invest intentionally instead of reactively
- Build buffers instead of relying on gallantry
- Make decisions from clarity, not urgency
- Plan deliberately for the future

This is where the organization stops borrowing energy from the founder and starts generating its own.

You are approaching readiness when each core offering works financially, cash flow is predictable, and you can explain where profit comes from — simply. That is not perfection. It is control and predictability. And control and predictability is what makes scale possible.

9.2. Strengthening Processes, Culture, and Client Retention

By this stage, one truth becomes unavoidable: Growth does not create problems. Growth reveals them.

What worked at ten customers begins to strain at fifty. What felt *"flexible"* starts to feel fragile. Loose systems, informal processes, unspoken cultural norms, and inconsistent client experiences surface under pressure.

<u>Stability is not achieved by adding more effort. It is achieved by tightening what already exists.</u>

From Systems to Processes: Making Execution Reliable

Earlier, we addressed the importance of identifying **key functions** and designing the **systems** that support them. This section builds on that foundation. Systems define *where* work lives. Processes define *how* work actually happens.

In the early stages, most processes live in people's heads. Founders know how things get done. Key team members *"just know."* Problems are solved through urgency, memory, and goodwill. That works — until volume exposes ambiguity.

Without clear processes:

- Ownership becomes unclear
- Quality varies by person
- Founders become default problem-solvers
- Decisions slow down unnecessarily

Strong processes do not reduce flexibility. They reduce confusion.

At this stage, the goal is not bureaucracy. It is clarity: clear handoffs; clear expectations; clear definitions of "done".

When processes stabilize, energy is freed — not constrained.

Culture Is What Shows Up Under Pressure

We've referenced culture earlier because it always exists. Here, it becomes visible. <u>Culture is not what is written. Culture is what happens when things are tight, when deadlines slip. When clients push back. When mistakes surface.</u>

I've worked with teams that spoke eloquently about values — yet rewarded behaviors that contradicted them. Over time, people stop listening to words and start watching patterns.

At this stage, stability requires alignment:

- What you prioritize becomes culture
- What you tolerate becomes culture
- What you reward becomes culture
- What you ignore becomes culture

This book does not attempt to fully unpack culture formation. That work is explored in depth in my book dedicated specifically to building, transforming, and sustaining organizational culture. Here, the focus is narrower: ensuring culture supports stability instead of undermining it.

Culture does not need to be loud. It needs to be consistent.

Client Retention Is a Leadership Discipline

Many founders chase new customers while quietly leaking existing ones. They invest heavily in acquisition but underinvest in experience. They track growth metrics but miss trust signals.

<u>Retention is rarely about price. It is about reliability.</u>

Clients stay when:

- Expectations are clear
- Delivery is consistent
- Communication is honest
- Problems are handled quickly and respectfully

Acquiring new clients is expensive — in time, money, and emotional energy. Retaining existing ones compounds quietly.

I learned this personally. At one point, I realized I was so focused on moving forward that I wasn't nurturing relationships already built. I changed course. I reached out to past clients — even those who had moved on. I expressed appreciation. I stayed connected without agenda. I've carried that principle into both business and life. Stability often grows from relationships you choose to honor, even when they no longer "serve" you directly.

Retention is not a tactic. It is a posture.

Where Stability Actually Comes From

Organizations stabilize when:

- Systems and processes reduce dependence on founders
- Culture reinforces the right behaviors under pressure
- Clients experience predictability, not surprises

This work is not glamorous. But it is foundational. And it is what allows profitability to last — not just appear.

In the next section, we examine what happens when instability persists — identifying bottlenecks, weak foundations, and growth barriers before they harden into permanent limits.

9.3. Fixing Bottlenecks, Weak Foundations, and Growth Barriers

Growth does not create problems. It reveals them.

What worked at ten customers strains at fifty. What felt flexible becomes fragile. Loose systems, informal processes, and unspoken norms surface under pressure. Stability is not achieved by more effort — it is achieved by tightening what already exists.

From Systems to Processes

Earlier, we focused on identifying core systems. Now the question is simpler: *How does work actually get done?*

In early stages, processes live in people's heads. Founders and early team members "just know." That works — until volume exposes ambiguity. Without clear processes:

- Ownership blurs
- Quality varies
- Founders become default problem-solvers

The goal here is not bureaucracy. It is clarity: clear handoffs, clear expectations, and clear definitions of "done." Strong processes reduce confusion, not flexibility.

Culture Shows Up Under Pressure

Culture is not what is written. It is what happens when deadlines slip, clients push back, or mistakes surface.

At this stage, culture becomes visible:

- What you prioritize becomes culture
- What you tolerate becomes culture
- What you reward becomes culture

Consistency matters more than slogans. Culture does not need to be loud. It needs to hold under pressure.

Client Retention Is a Leadership Discipline

Many founders chase new clients while quietly losing existing ones. Retention is rarely about price. It is about reliability.

<u>Clients stay when expectations are clear, delivery is consistent, communication is honest, and problems are handled quickly.</u>

I learned this personally when I realized I was moving forward without nurturing relationships already built. I changed course — reconnecting with past clients without agenda. That discipline carried forward. Stability often grows from relationships you choose to honor, even when they no longer "serve" you directly.

Retention is not a tactic. It is a posture.

Where Stability Comes From

Organizations stabilize when:

- Processes reduce dependence on heroism
- Culture reinforces the right behaviors under pressure
- Clients experience predictability, not surprises

This work is not glamorous. But it is what allows profitability to last — not just appear.

In the next section, we examine what happens when instability persists — and how to identify bottlenecks before they harden into permanent limits.

9.4. Scale Readiness Assessment (what investors and acquirers look for)

Many founders mistake momentum for readiness. Revenue is rising. People are busy. Opportunities are increasing. But *scale readiness is not emotional — it is structural.*

Investors and acquirers look for evidence that growth can occur ***without breaking the organization.***

How Serious Investors Think About Scale

As **Adam Coffey** explains, disciplined investors outperform not by working harder, but by structuring companies for repeatable execution. While many owner-led businesses aim for modest annual returns, professional operators pursue far higher returns by designing for margin expansion, operational leverage, and predictable performance.

Scale, in this context, is engineered — not hoped for. Capital follows organizations that can execute growth systematically, not just pursue it enthusiastically.

Scaling Is Also a Cash Conversation

Growth stresses cash before it relieves it. More customers often mean higher payroll, longer collection cycles, and tighter working capital. Investors know this. Acquirers look for it.

Scale readiness includes the ability to fund growth calmly — without panic, blind borrowing, or starving operations. Growth you cannot finance or control is not leverage. It is risk.

Growth vs. Scale

Growth means doing more.
Scale means doing more **without proportionally increasing strain**.

True scale shows up when:

- Output increases faster than effort
- Decisions move closer to the work
- Systems replace constant intervention
- Results become predictable, not volatile

If everything still runs through the founder, the organization maybe growing — not scaling.

What External Evaluators Look For

Across investors, partners, and acquirers, the signals are consistent:

- **Clarity:** Is the value proposition clear and repeatable?
- **Consistency:** Are results dependent on systems or people?
- **Control:** Are financials, metrics, and risks visible?
- **Independence:** Can the organization function without constant founder involvement?

Hype does not substitute for structure.

Common Signals Scale Is Premature

Expansion should pause when patterns like these persist:

- Founder-centered decision-making
- Unclear or inconsistent margins
- Growth without documentation or process
- High acquisition with weak retention
- Culture held together by personality instead of standards

These are not failures. They are signals to stabilize first.

Scale Readiness Is Earned Early

Organizations that scale well:

- Stabilize before expanding
- Repair foundations before accelerating
- Choose clarity over speed
- Address constraints instead of pushing past them

If growth feels heavy now, it will feel unmanageable later.

Reflect & Practice
Reflection Prompts

- Where does growth currently feel heavier instead of lighter in your organization?
- Which systems, decisions, or processes still depend too heavily on you?
- What foundation, if strengthened now, would remove the greatest future constraint?

Practice Challenge (7 Days)

Over the next week:

- Identify one recurring bottleneck that slows progress.
- Trace it back to its root cause — not the symptom.
- Make one small structural adjustment to reduce dependence, friction, or rework.

Scale readiness is not about expansion. It is about alignment.

You have now moved from launch to stability. What comes next is intentional expansion — scaling with control, coherence, and long-term value in mind.

PART IV

SCALE & EXIT

"Scaling is not about doing more. It is about doing what matters, better."
Alvin Toffler, Business Expert, Author, and Entrepreneur

Grow strategically. Multiply wisely. Prepare and scale with intention. Build something that outlasts you. Exit Successfully.

G rowth and scale are often treated as synonyms. They are not. Growth is expansion. Scale is multiplication without proportional strain. By this stage, the question is no longer *Can this work?* The harder question is: *Can this work without me holding everything together?* That question changes everything.

Scale Amplifies What You Tolerate

Scale exposes what earlier stages could absorb. What felt manageable at ten clients becomes painful at one hundred. What felt flexible at five employees becomes chaotic at fifty.

Across venture-backed and private-equity-backed companies, breakdowns at scale are rarely caused by market failure. They are caused by internal fragility — leadership bottlenecks, weak systems, and cultural drift that were never corrected when the organization was smaller.

Scale does not create problems. It amplifies what already exists.

Why Organizations Break at Scale

Scaling failures usually come from misalignment:

- Systems that were never designed to repeat
- Leaders who were never developed to delegate
- Culture that worked informally but collapsed under pressure
- Business models that produced revenue but not resilience
- Founders who remained indispensable instead of replaceable

Growth arrived before readiness. Scale must be earned, not rushed.

Scale Is a Design Problem

Founders often believe scaling requires more drive and more hustle. In reality, scale requires less feat and more discipline:

- Repeatable systems instead of improvisation
- Clear decision rights instead of constant escalation
- Leadership layers instead of founder dependency
- Financial clarity instead of hope-based growth
- Cultural standards instead of personality-driven norms

Scale is not about doing everything bigger. It is about doing fewer things consistently — without you.

Why Investors Care About Stability First

Sophisticated investors do not invest in growth alone. They invest in controlled growth. Many distressed-but-growing companies attract capital only after founders lose leverage. Savvy operators stabilize systems, restore margins, professionalize leadership, and then scale or exit profitably. The difference is not intelligence. It is readiness. Investors are not asking whether your company can grow. They are asking whether it can *hold* what it grows.

And not all capital is the same.

Not All Capital Is the Same — And That Matters

Founders often talk about "raising capital" as if it were a single decision. It is not. <u>Different forms of capital come with different expectations, timelines, pressures, and consequences.</u> Understanding the capital pathway early is part of designing an organization that can scale — or exit — on its own terms.

At a high level, most founders encounter capital across distinct stages:

- **Angel Investors**
  Individuals investing personal capital, typically at the idea or early validation stage. Angels provide seed funding, early belief, and sometimes mentorship — but capital is limited and informal.
- **Venture Capital (Series A, B, C)**
  Institutional investors funding high-growth startups with the expectation of rapid scale and eventual liquidity through acquisition or IPO. Venture capital accelerates growth — and scrutiny.
- **Syndications and Small Funds**
  Groups of investors pooling capital to acquire or invest in small to mid-sized businesses. Common in acquisition entrepreneurship and early roll-up strategies.
- **Private Equity**
  Firms that acquire mature, cash-flowing businesses. Private equity prioritizes operational discipline, margin expansion, and eventual exit — often with leadership replacement already assumed.
- **Growth Capital (A Newer Path)**
  Institutional capital designed for companies that want to scale significantly without going public or issuing an IPO. Growth capital allows large, profitable, or near-profitable private

companies to remain private for extended periods — often a decade or more — without short-term performance pressure.

Growth capital has enabled companies like **Stripe** to delay or avoid IPOs entirely, preserving long-term decision-making, founder influence, and strategic flexibility. Unlike traditional venture or public markets, these investors are often patient, aligned with durability, and willing to wait for value creation rather than demand quarterly results.

The point is not that one path is better than another. The point is that *capital choice shapes organizational behavior*.

Designing systems, leadership, governance, and incentives without understanding the likely capital path often leads to misalignment later — when leverage is lower and options are fewer. Founders who understand these pathways early design organizations that remain attractive to *multiple* forms of capital — or none at all.

That optionality is what scale is meant to create.

Optionality Is the Real Goal

This part of the book is not about size for its own sake. It is about optionality — the ability to choose:

1. Grow without burnout
2. Raise capital without losing control
3. Step back without collapse
4. Sell, merge, license, or exit by choice — not pressure
5. Decide what comes next

Organizations that scale well give founders options. Organizations that scale poorly take them away.

Scaling Happens in Stages (Even If You Exit Early)

Some founders do not intend to scale the company themselves. They plan to launch, prove demand, then sell, recapitalize, or bring in investors. That is still a scaling conversation, because buyers and investors pay for *scalability* — the ability to grow without rebuilding the foundation.

In practice, scaling is experienced in stages, where new constraints appear and new disciplines are required. The exact thresholds vary by industry, but the pattern is common:

- **Pre-revenue to $1M**: Prove demand, tighten delivery, stabilize cash discipline.
- **$1M to $3M-$5M**: Remove founder bottlenecks, standardize operations, build basic leadership capacity.
- **$5M to $10M**: Install operating rhythms, strengthen middle leadership, tighten metrics and accountability.
- **$10M to $30M+**: Build real governance, deepen management layers, strengthen margins, reduce key-person risk.
- **$30M to $100M+**: Scale becomes institutional — systems, decision quality, culture, and capital discipline determine outcomes.

<u>This book does not attempt to teach every late-stage tactic across every revenue band.</u> It gives you the *end-to-end framework* that makes each stage possible: design for transferability, form with discipline, launch with learning, stabilize for profitability, and scale with systems and leadership that can survive beyond the founder.

What Part IV Will Help You Do

In this final part, you will learn how to:

- Evaluate scaling paths and choose intentionally
- Strengthen systems, leadership, and culture for growth
- Decide when — and when not — to use capital
- Avoid common scaling traps
- Prepare early for exit, even if leaving is not the plan

This is not about building something bigger at all costs. It is about building something strong enough to endure growth.

Scale Is Not the Finish Line

Scale is a threshold, not a destination. What comes after — leadership transfer, partial exit, full exit, reinvention, or legacy-building — depends entirely on how well the organization was prepared.

The goal was never just to build something that grows. ***It was to build something that lasts*** — and gives you the freedom to choose what comes next.

Chapter 10
Choose Your Scaling Vehicles

"Scale is not a goal. Scale is a consequence." **Jeff Bezos,** Founder of
Amazon

**Explore scaling pathways. Consider alternatives.
Choose strategically. Scale in ways aligned with your
mission.**

Scaling is not a single decision. It is a series of choices made over
time. By this stage, the organization has customers, revenue,
systems, and a track record. The question is no longer whether
it can grow, but how it should grow — and at what cost.

This is where many founders hesitate. Growth feels inevitable.
Investors expect it. Advisors encourage it. Peers celebrate it. Yet few
pause to ask the more important question: *What kind of scale actually fits
this organization — and my life?* There is no universal answer. There are
only informed choices.

Founders face many potential scaling paths — pricing, products,
people, capital, partnerships, acquisitions, geography, platforms,
licensing, and more. This chapter does not attempt to catalog them
all. It focuses on the most common and consequential scaling
vehicles — and the discipline required to choose among them.

Scaling Is a Strategic Choice

One of the most damaging assumptions in entrepreneurship is that
success automatically requires aggressive expansion. I have worked
with founders who scaled too early or too broadly and lost control of
quality, culture, or health. I have also worked with founders who

chose focused, restrained scaling and built durable, profitable organizations that served them well for decades. Both paths can work. The risk lies in unexamined growth. Scaling is not about size. It is about leverage. The right scaling vehicle allows you to:

1. Serve more people without proportional effort
2. Increase impact without burnout
3. Grow value without increasing fragility

The wrong vehicle does the opposite. <u>Most scaling failures happen not because founders lack commitment, but because they choose the wrong vehicle at the wrong time</u> — adding complexity before leverage or reach before readiness.

Multiple Paths — One Discipline

Scaling is not a formula. As **Adam Coffey's** work shows, organizations scale through different paths depending on industry dynamics and leadership maturity — operational optimization, margin expansion, organic growth, acquisitions, or geographic expansion. What matters is not the path itself, but the discipline behind it. Organizations that scale well know which *levers* matter most at their stage and resist pursuing every opportunity at once. Scale is not acceleration in all directions. It is focused amplification.

What This Chapter Will Help You Do

This chapter introduces the primary scaling vehicles available to founders — internal and external — and the tradeoffs each one carries. *The goal is not to push you toward scale, but to help you choose deliberately rather than accidentally.* You will explore how organizations scale by:

- Deepening what they already control
- Expanding leadership and decision-making capacity
- Using capital, partnerships, or acquisitions wisely

- Aligning scaling choices with mission, values, and life goals

Scale should strengthen what you've built — not strain it. The founders who succeed at this stage are not the ones who chase every opportunity. They are the ones who *choose their scaling vehicles with intention.*

10.1. Internal Scaling Options

Internal scaling focuses on expanding capacity and value *using what the organization already controls.* It is about going *deeper* before going wider — and it is often the most sustainable path to scale.

Many founders assume scale requires something external: new markets, new capital, or new products. In reality, many organizations have untapped leverage already inside their walls. Internal scaling asks one essential question: **How much more value can we create from what we already have?**

Below are the primary internal scaling vehicles founders use, often in combination.

1. Scaling Through Systems and Processes

This is the foundation of internal scale. Systems allow output to grow without proportional effort. Effective internal scaling through systems includes:

- Standardizing delivery and workflows
- Clarifying ownership and handoffs
- Reducing rework and decision friction
- Removing founder dependency from execution

This is not bureaucracy. It is repeatability. <u>When systems work, growth feels lighter instead of heavier.</u>

2. Scaling Through Pricing and Margin Expansion

Pricing is one of the fastest and most underused internal levers. Internal pricing scale includes:

- Raising prices on proven offers
- Simplifying delivery while preserving outcomes
- Eliminating underpriced or high-friction services

Higher margins create cash, flexibility, and room to invest. Thin margins do not scale. Price discipline is not greed — it is stability.

3. Scaling Through People and Leadership Capacity

Hiring alone does not create scale. Empowerment does. People-based internal scaling focuses on:

- Expanding decision authority beyond the founder
- Developing leaders who own outcomes
- Clarifying roles tied to value creation

Sometimes this requires new hires. Often, it requires unlocking capacity already present.

4. Scaling Through Capacity and Efficiency

Many organizations try to grow outward while operating below true capacity. Internal efficiency scale includes:

- Improving utilization of existing resources
- Reducing waste, delays, and bottlenecks
- Increasing throughput without adding headcount

Often, the fastest path to growth is inward.

5. Scaling Through Geographic Replication (Carefully)

Geographic expansion works internally only when:

- Knowledge lives in processes, not people
- Quality does not depend on founder presence
- Culture is taught, not assumed
- Leadership exists beyond headquarters

Without this readiness, expansion amplifies inconsistency instead of value.

6. Scaling Through Focus and Simplification

Internal scale often comes from doing less:

- Narrowing to the most profitable offers
- Eliminating low-margin distractions
- Concentrating resources on what compounds

Complexity feels like progress. Focus creates scale.

Internal Scale Comes First

Internal scaling builds margins, leadership depth, repeatability, and resilience. Without these, external scale becomes fragile. Strong organizations use internal scale to *earn the right* to scale outward.

In the next section, we examine external scaling options — capital, partnerships, acquisitions, and platforms — and how to evaluate when they truly make sense.

10.2. External Scaling Options

External scaling expands capacity by leveraging assets you do not fully own — capital, partners, platforms, or other organizations' infrastructure. When used well, it accelerates growth. When used poorly, it magnifies fragility. External scale should answer one clear question: *What constraint does this remove — and at what cost?*

Below are the primary external scaling vehicles founders consider.

1. Scaling Through Capital

Capital is not a strategy. It is an accelerant. External capital may come from investors, private equity, debt, or strategic partners. It is typically used to:

- Upgrade systems and infrastructure
- Hire key leaders or teams
- Implement technology
- Fund expansion or distribution

The risk is using money to compensate for weak fundamentals. Capital does not fix broken systems, unclear pricing, or founder bottlenecks — it scales them faster. Well-run organizations raise capital to expand what already works, not to rescue what doesn't.

2. Scaling Through Partnerships and Joint Ventures

Partnerships scale by combining strengths instead of duplicating effort. This includes:

- Strategic partnerships
- Joint ventures
- Licensing or channel relationships

Partnerships fail most often due to ambiguity, not bad intent. External scale through partners works only when:

- Goals and positioning are clear
- Standards are documented
- Decision rights are defined
- Accountability is enforced

Done well, partnerships extend reach efficiently. Done poorly, they dilute brand, culture, and trust.

3. Scaling Through Acquisition

Acquisition compresses time — and front-loads complexity. It works best when:

- The core business model is proven
- Leadership and integration capacity exist
- Systems can absorb complexity
- Culture fit is evaluated honestly

Acquisitions scale in two primary ways:

- **Vertical** – strengthening control over suppliers or distribution
- **Horizontal** – expanding market reach or capabilities

Private equity succeeds here by stabilizing first, then acquiring with discipline. <u>Acquisition is not a shortcut for weak fundamentals.</u> It is an accelerator for strong ones.

10.3. Digital Scaling Options (One-to-many Leverage)

External scaling adds resources. Digital scaling changes the economics of growth. <u>Instead of increasing output by adding people, locations, or coordination, digital scale multiplies impact without proportional increases in cost or effort.</u> When designed well, it turns insight into infrastructure.

Digital scale is not about "going online." It is about *decoupling growth from marginal effort.*

What Digital Scaling Actually Is

Digital scaling converts what already works into formats that travel farther with less friction, such as:

- Digital products and programs
- Subscriptions or memberships
- Platforms or ecosystems
- Content-driven demand engines
- Licensing intellectual property

The common thread is simple: ***one act of creation enables many acts of value delivery***. Many founders exhaust themselves delivering the same insight repeatedly, one client at a time, when a digital format could extend reach without sacrificing quality. Digital scale does not remove human connection — it preserves it while expanding access.

Where Digital Scale Breaks Down

Digital scale is powerful — and unforgiving. It fails when founders assume:

- Promotion can replace clarity
- Volume will fix weak design
- Tools can substitute for systems

Effective digital scale requires:

- Clear value articulation
- Designed customer pathways
- Consistent delivery standards
- Tight feedback loops

Without these, digital scale multiplies confusion instead of value.

Repeatable Pathways Create Leverage

Digital scale works through designed pathways, not constant effort. Organizations that scale digitally build clear flows from awareness to value, and from value to commitment. When pathways are visible, growth becomes predictable instead of exhausting.

Digital scale works best when:

- The core offer is already proven
- Outcomes are clearly defined
- Delivery can be standardized without losing integrity

Digital Scale Is a Choice, Not a Requirement

Not every organization should scale digitally — but every founder should evaluate it deliberately. When aligned, digital scale can:

- Increase margins
- Reduce founder dependency
- Expand reach without organizational bloat
- Create optionality for licensing, platforms, or exit

When misaligned, it simply creates noise at volume. The question is not whether digital scale is possible. It is whether it fits the organization you are building.

In the next section, we examine how strong organizations combine internal, external, and digital scaling — and what the most successful scaled companies consistently get right.

10.4. Case Studies of Scaled Companies

Scaling does not follow a single formula. These organizations succeeded not because they grew quickly, but because they aligned *how* they scaled with what they controlled and what they were disciplined enough to protect. These cases are not models to copy. They are reference points — illustrating distinct scaling vehicles in practice across industries and regions.

Representative Scaling Paths

1. Internal Process Scale

Toyota (Japan)

Scaling vehicle: Internal systems and operational excellence. Toyota scaled through disciplined systems, not speed. Expansion followed only after processes proved repeatable across locations and cultures.

Lesson: If systems cannot scale, growth will expose you.

2. Platform and Ecosystem Scale

Amazon (United States)

Scaling vehicle: Platform infrastructure. Amazon scaled by enabling others — sellers, developers, partners — to create value within its ecosystem.

Lesson: Scale accelerates when coordination outpaces ownership.

3. Brand-Led Replicatio

Starbucks (United States)

Scaling vehicle: Repeatable brand experience. Starbucks scaled through consistency — training, standards, and experience — with limited local adaptation.

Lesson: Brand scales only when discipline backs it.

4. Standardization with Local Adaptation

IKEA (Europe)

Scaling vehicle: Fixed core with flexible edges. IKEA standardized design and cost discipline while allowing local adaptation around a stable backbone.

Lesson: Scale works when the core stays fixed and the edges flex.

5. Infrastructure-Led Scale

Safaricom (M-Pesa) – Africa

Scaling vehicle: Infrastructure and trust. M-Pesa scaled by solving a fundamental problem simply and reliably, becoming embedded infrastructure rather than a product.

Lesson: Trust compounds faster than sophistication.

6. Marketplace Platform Scale

Alibaba Group (Asia)

Scaling vehicle: Ecosystem orchestration. Alibaba scaled by coordinating sellers, logistics, and services without owning most assets.

Lesson: Platforms scale fastest when ownership is distributed and governance is strong.

Synthesis: Scaling Vehicles at a Glance

Company	Primary Scaling Vehicle	Core Discipline Enabling Scale
Toyota	Internal systems & processes	Operational excellence & repeatability
Amazon	Platform & ecosystem	Infrastructure before speed
Starbucks	Brand replication	Training & experience consistency
IKEA	Standardization with local adaptation	Cost discipline & design clarity
Safaricom	Infrastructure + partnerships	Trust & relevance
Alibaba	Marketplace platform	Ecosystem coordination

What These Cases Have in Common

Despite different industries and regions, these companies share a few fundamentals:

- They **chose a scaling vehicle deliberately**
- They **built systems before speed**
- They **aligned scale with identity** — not ego
- They **designed for transferability, not founder dependence**

There is no single "right" way to scale. But there is a wrong one: *growing without intention.*

Reflect & Practice

Reflection Prompts

- Which scaling vehicle best fits how your organization actually creates value?
- Which example created resistance — and what does that reveal?
- If demand doubled tomorrow, what would strain first?

Practice Challenge (7 Days)

- Identify the one scaling vehicle you are most drawn to — and why.
- Identify one vehicle you should avoid for now — and why.
- Have one focused conversation with an advisor about *how* you want to scale, not just *how fast.*

Scale does not begin with expansion. It begins with selection.

In Chapter 11, we turn to what determines whether scale holds — the leadership, discipline, and operating behaviors that prevent growth from collapsing under its own weight.

Chapter 11

Principles, Disciplines, & Best Practices of Sustained Scale

"Success is not built on success. It is built on failure, frustration, and learning."
Sumner Redstone, Businessman and Media Magnate

Sustain the scale. Reduce founder dependence. Build leadership depth. Prepare for exit.

Scaling exposes truth. It reveals what was designed deliberately — and what was merely tolerated. By the time an organization reaches this stage, growth is no longer a theory or a goal. The scaling vehicles chosen in the previous chapter have been deployed. Customers have increased. Revenue is flowing. Complexity has arrived. Decisions now carry weight. Mistakes cost more — financially, culturally, and personally.

This is where many founders experience an unexpected tension. On paper, the organization looks successful. In practice, everything feels heavier than it should. More coordination. More exceptions. More dependence on a few people. That tension is not failure. It is feedback.

Early growth rewards energy, improvisation, and responsiveness. Sustained scale does not. At scale, effort alone becomes expensive. What once worked through proximity now requires consistency. What once relied on intuition must now be supported by principles and discipline — not discipline as rigidity, but discipline as reliability.

This chapter sits at a critical inflection point in the journey. It is the bridge between *scaling* and *exit*.

Choosing the right scaling vehicle is only the beginning. What determines long-term success — and exit readiness — is whether the organization can *hold* that scale without breaking. Investors, buyers, and successors are no longer asking, *"Can this company grow?"* They are asking, *"Can this company sustain growth without the founder holding everything together?"*

This chapter focuses on what makes scale endure:

- The operating principles that stabilize complexity.
- The disciplines that replace valor with predictability.
- The leadership depth, behaviors, and cultural reinforcement required to prevent growth from collapsing under its own weight.

Sustained scale is not about adding more. It is about strengthening what already exists — so the organization can grow, adapt, and eventually transition without losing its integrity or value. The founders who master this stage do not just build bigger organizations. They exit successfully. They build organizations that can outlast them.

11.1. From Scaling Vehicles to Sustained Scale: Testing What You Built

Choosing a scaling vehicle is not the finish line. It is the start of accountability. By this stage, scale is no longer theoretical. Systems have been stressed. Capital deployed. Leaders added. Partnerships formed. Revenue increased — along with complexity. The critical question now is not *whether* the organization has grown, but *how* it has grown.

Is the chosen scaling vehicle creating leverage — or just more activity?

Scale rarely fails loudly at first. It fails quietly: through friction, unclear decisions, creeping founder dependence, and systems that work only when pressure is low. Sustained scale begins by testing what was built.

What Sustained Scale Requires

Growth at this stage must meet three conditions:

1. Performance improves without proportional effort
2. Decisions move downward, not upward
3. Results repeat without founder presence

If revenue rises but stress, fragility, or founder involvement rise with it, the organization has expanded — not scaled. Sustained scale is not momentum. It is *durability*.

Common Warning Signs After Scaling

When scale is unstable, patterns repeat:

- Systems exist but are bypassed under pressure
- Leaders are named but authority is unclear
- Capital was raised but outcomes are diffuse
- Partnerships lack accountability
- Tools are digital, but workflows remain manual
- Founders remain the default decision-maker

These are not execution problems. They are design failures — signals that scaling vehicles were deployed without the disciplines required to sustain them.

Make Leverage Visible

The first discipline of sustained scale is visibility. Founders must answer honestly:

- What now works without me?
- Where did leverage actually increase?

- Where did complexity increase without payoff?
- What breaks when I step away?

<u>Scale that cannot be explained cannot be transferred. And scale that cannot be transferred cannot be exited.</u>

From Founder Energy to Operating Principles

Early growth runs on energy. *Sustained scale runs on principles.* At this stage, organizations must replace intuition with shared rules:

- How decisions are made
- Who owns outcomes
- What standards are non-negotiable
- How exceptions are handled

These are not values statements. They are **operating guardrails**. Without them, scale depends on personality. With them, scale becomes institutional.

Why This Comes Before Leadership and Exit

Conversations about succession, valuation, or exit are premature if scale itself is unstable. Investors and acquirers do not ask first about growth rate. They ask whether the organization can hold what it has built. This section draws a clear line:

- Scale that is not sustained becomes a liability
- Scale that is sustained becomes an asset

The next sections focus on *reinforcing scale* — through leadership, behavior, and systems — so the organization no longer depends on the founder to survive its own success.

11.2. Leadership Depth, Delegation, and Successor Readiness

Scale becomes sustainable only when leadership expands faster than complexity. At this stage, the organization no longer needs more effort from the founder. <u>It needs judgment distributed across the system.</u> As scale increases, decisions multiply, context stretches, and founder involvement becomes a constraint rather than an advantage. *Delegation is no longer optional — it is existential.*

Delegation Is Ownership, Not Task Transfer

Most founders believe they have delegated because work has moved off their plate. In reality, they often retain decision authority. True delegation requires three elements to move together:

- **Responsibility** – Who owns the outcome
- **Authority** – Who decides without escalation
- **Accountability** – How results are measured

When one is missing, decisions drift upward and dependency quietly returns. Sustained scale requires founders to shift from solving problems to designing decision environments.

Leadership Depth Is the Real Scale Multiplier

Investors and acquirers do not ask whether the founder can lead. They ask who leads when the founder is absent. An organization is not scale-ready if:

- Strategic decisions depend on one person
- Client relationships collapse without founder presence
- Hiring, performance, or escalation bottleneck upward
- No one can explain how decisions are made without approval

<u>Leadership depth is not about titles. It is about independent judgment operating within clear boundaries.</u>

Successor Readiness Is a System, Not a Person

Succession does not begin with naming a replacement. It begins with structure. Regardless of who eventually steps in, three conditions must already exist:

1. Strategy is explicit, not intuitive
2. Decision rights are documented, not assumed
3. Performance standards are enforced consistently

Without these, no successor can succeed — and buyers know it. Strong founders quietly build successor readiness early by expanding authority, exposure, and accountability across two or three potential leaders. Through real decisions and controlled risk, the organization reveals who can carry weight.

Developing Leaders for Scale

A common failure at this stage is assuming capable managers will automatically scale. Many struggle with ambiguity, cross-functional judgment, and peer accountability. High-performing organizations invest deliberately in:

- Coaching and mentoring for senior leaders
- Clear escalation and decision frameworks
- Feedback systems that reward judgment, not compliance

Leadership does not scale with revenue. It must be developed.

What External Evaluators Look For

Investors and acquirers assess one core question: Can this organization function without the founder?

They look for:

- Leaders who articulate strategy clearly
- Decisions made close to the work
- Predictable performance across functions
- Evidence of internal leadership continuity

When leadership depth is real, valuation increases. When it is missing, growth becomes a liability.

From Control to Trust

The final shift here is psychological. Founders must move from controlling outcomes to trusting systems and people to produce them. This does not lower standards — it enforces them structurally rather than personally. Sustained scale depends on leaders who can carry weight — and founders willing to let them.

In the next section, we focus on the behaviors, cultural disciplines, and operating rhythms that protect scale under pressure once leadership is distributed.

11.3. Culture, Discipline, and Decision Quality at Scale

At small scale, culture is shaped by proximity. At scale, it is shaped by defaults. When founders are no longer present in every decision, culture becomes whatever the organization falls back on under pressure. At this stage, culture is no longer what leaders say. It is how decisions are made when no one is watching. Discipline becomes the invisible operating system that protects execution, judgment, and trust.

From Personality to Principle

Early culture often lives inside the founder — tone, urgency, values-in-action. That model breaks at scale. *Sustained growth requires culture to move from personality to principle.* Scaled cultures are:

- Explicit, not implied

- Embedded in systems, not speeches
- Protected through consequences, not reminders

Organizations that scale well translate beliefs into decision criteria, operating principles, and non-negotiable standards. Culture becomes executable, not aspirational.

Discipline Replaces Founder Control

As authority is delegated, discipline must replace control. Without it, delegation creates drift instead of leverage. Discipline shows up in:

- How decisions are made and reviewed
- How priorities are set and protected
- How exceptions are handled
- How underperformance is addressed

<u>High-performing organizations are not rigid — they are predictable.</u> People know what good looks like, where decisions belong, and what happens when standards slip. That clarity reduces friction even as complexity increases.

Decision Quality Is the True Growth Multiplier

At scale, outcomes depend less on individual brilliance and more on collective decision quality. Poor decisions compound faster than good ones. Weak calls spread. Bad incentives persist. Mature organizations invest in:

- Clear decision rights
- Defined escalation paths
- Post-decision reviews
- Learning without blame

Scale rewards judgment, not daring. Teams with consistent decision discipline often outperform more "talented" teams that lack clarity and accountability.

What External Evaluators Look For

At this stage, buyers and investors are asking:

- Does culture travel without the founder?
- Are standards enforced consistently?
- Do leaders make aligned decisions under pressure?
- Is discipline embedded or manually enforced?

Organizations that pass this test feel calm, even while growing. Those that fail feel noisy, political, and fragile — regardless of revenue. *Sustained scale depends on culture that holds, discipline that travels, and decision quality that improves with size* — not degrades.

In the next section, we focus on how organizations institutionalize learning and accountability so scale strengthens over time instead of unraveling quietly.

11.4. Scale That Holds vs. Scale That Breaks (Success and Failure Patterns)

Scale reveals character — organizational and personal. At this stage, outcomes diverge sharply. Some organizations absorb growth and become stronger. Others fracture under the weight of what they failed to institutionalize. The difference is rarely intelligence, market opportunity, or access to capital. It is discipline.

When Scale Holds

Organizations that sustain scale share a consistent pattern:

- Leadership depth exists beyond the founder
- Decision authority is clear and enforced

- Systems carry load instead of bombast
- Culture is reinforced through behavior, not slogans
- Governance evolves as complexity increases

These organizations treat growth as responsibility, not celebration. As success rises, discipline tightens. Assumptions are challenged. Feedback travels upward. Scale becomes leverage — not fragility.

Microsoft (US)

When Bill Gates stepped away from day-to-day leadership, Microsoft did not weaken — it stabilized and later reaccelerated. Strategy was explicit, leadership succession intentional, and governance independent of the founder. The company remained valuable because it no longer depended on him.

Inditex (Europe)

Inditex scaled globally through tightly designed systems, fast decision loops, and distributed execution. Founder Amancio Ortega stepped back without destabilizing the business because leadership, process, and accountability were already institutionalized.

MercadoLibre (South America)

MercadoLibre scaled across volatile markets by building logistics, payments, and marketplace infrastructure before chasing speed. Governance and local autonomy were established early, allowing growth without operational collapse.

In each case, scale held because success was designed to outlive the founder.

When Scale Breaks

Failure at scale is usually quieter — and more predictable. Common breakdown patterns include:

- Founders refusing to release control

- Early success hardening into arrogance
- Systems lagging behind growth
- Cultural standards bent "just this once"
- Warning signs dismissed because results still look good

These organizations grow, but they do not mature. Scale magnifies denial.

Quibi (US)
Despite capital, brand power, and talent, Quibi failed because execution discipline, feedback loops, and adaptability were missing. Capital accelerated collapse instead of preventing it.

WeWork (US)
WeWork scaled valuation and footprint without institutionalizing governance, leadership independence, or operational discipline. When scrutiny arrived, valuation collapsed. The issue was not lack of value. It was founder centrality.

Nokia (Europe)
Nokia's decline stemmed from delayed decisions, internal silos, and cultural rigidity. Scale existed, but learning and leadership discipline did not keep pace with market shifts.

These companies grew. They did not mature.

The Real Divider

The line between scale that holds and scale that breaks is institutionalization:

- Did leadership become distributable?
- Were standards enforced consistently?
- Was governance strengthened before it was required?
- Did humility survive success?

Organizations that answer yes earn credibility at scale. Those that do not may still grow — but they grow brittle.

Reflect & Practice
Reflection Prompts

- Where does execution still rely on informal bravery?
- Which decisions are escalated today that should already be owned elsewhere?
- If you stepped away for 90 days, what would weaken first?

Practice Challenge (14 Days)

- Identify one recurring issue from the past year.
- Document its root cause, accountable owner, and corrective standard.
- Assign ownership and set a 30-day review — without founder intervention.

When scale holds, systems carry load, leaders absorb pressure, and performance persists without constant founder presence. At that point, exit is no longer a rescue plan — it becomes an option.

Chapter 12 shifts from sustaining scale to understanding exit paths — where durable leadership, transferable value, and governance turn scale into freedom.

Chapter 12
Exit — Strategy, Preparation, Execution, & Life After Exit

"A great exit is not the end of a journey. It is the beginning of your next chapter." **Howard Schultz**, Founder of Starbucks

Prepare early. Execute wisely. Transition deliberately. Leave something that outlasts you.

The work of scaling does not end when growth stabilizes. It ends when the organization can endure *without you.*

Chapter 11 focused on what allows scale to hold — the principles, disciplines, leadership depth, and institutional behaviors that prevent growth from collapsing under its own weight. When those elements are in place, something profound happens: the business stops being an extension of the founder and starts becoming an entity in its own right. That moment is not an ending. It is the beginning of *exit readiness.*

Most founders misunderstand exit. They think of it as a transaction — something you consider only when you are tired, wealthy, or ready to move on. Others avoid it entirely, believing that planning an exit signals disloyalty to the mission or lack of long-term commitment. Both views are incomplete — and dangerous.

Exit is not a decision you make at the end of the journey. It is a condition your organization reaches through years of deliberate design. Whether or not you intend to sell, merge, step back, or go public, your organization is either *exit-ready* or it is not. And that readiness determines far more than financial outcomes. It determines resilience, continuity, legacy, and choice.

Exit Thinking Matters — Even If You Never Plan to Leave

One of the most uncomfortable truths in leadership is this: *life does not ask for permission.* Founders are sometimes forced to exit not because they want to, but because circumstances demand it. Death. Health crises. Accidents. Divorce. Partner disputes. Burnout. Regulatory changes. Market shocks. Family obligations. Shifts in values or priorities.

I have seen founders lose decades of work because they were forced into an exit they never prepared for. I have also seen founders navigate unexpected transitions with dignity and strength — not because they were lucky, but because they had built organizations that could survive their absence. ***The difference was not intelligence. It was intentionality.***

Organizations that are not designed for exit tend to unravel under pressure. Decisions stall. Trust erodes. Value leaks. Buyers sense dependency and negotiate aggressively. Employees feel uncertainty. What could have been a thoughtful transition becomes a rushed liquidation — often at a fraction of true value. <u>This is how founders end up exiting for pennies on the dollar — not because the business lacked potential, but because it lacked preparedness.</u>

Exit as a Leadership Responsibility

Designing for exit is not about leaving. *It is about stewardship.* When you design an organization that can be sold, transferred, merged, or stepped away from, you are doing more than protecting yourself financially. You are protecting:

- Employees who depend on continuity
- Customers who depend on reliability

- Partners and investors who depend on clarity
- A mission that deserves to outlive its creator

Paradoxically, the founders who plan for exit earliest are often the ones who stay longest — because they build companies that no longer trap them. Exit readiness creates *optionality*. Optionality creates leverage. Leverage creates freedom. And freedom is what allows founders to choose what comes next — rather than being forced into decisions by circumstance.

What This Chapter Is — and Is Not

This chapter is not about rushing toward a sale. It is not about optimizing vanity valuations. It is not about abandoning what you built. It *is* about understanding the exit paths available to you, the conditions required for each, and the behaviors that determine whether an exit becomes a reward — or a regret.

You will explore:

- The most common exit strategies and what they demand of the organization
- How buyers, investors, and successors actually evaluate readiness
- Why some founders exit cleanly while others stumble — even with strong businesses
- What life after exit really looks like, beyond the headlines and checks

Most importantly, this chapter reframes exit as the *final discipline of leadership* — not a betrayal of it. If scale was about building something bigger than you, exit is about building something that does not need you. And when that is done well, the story does not end.

It evolves.

12.1. Exit Strategies — Choosing the Right Path

There is no single "best" exit. There is only the right exit for *this organization, at this stage, in this season of your life.*

One of the most common founder mistakes is treating exit as a single outcome — usually selling the company. In reality, exit is a **set of strategic choices**, each with different implications for control, risk, legacy, and identity. Founders who choose an exit without understanding its requirements often feel disappointed — even when the check clears.

This section is about clarity before tactics.

Exit Is an Alignment Decision

An exit path must align four realities:

1. **Founder goals** – financial, emotional, lifestyle, purpose
2. **Organizational maturity** – systems, leadership, independence
3. **Stakeholder expectations** – partners, investors, employees
4. **Market reality** – buyer appetite, industry norms, timing

Misalignment in any one creates friction later — often when leverage is lowest. Founders who exit well choose deliberately. Founders who exit poorly drift into one.

The Primary Exit Paths

1. Selling to a Strategic or Financial Buyer
The most common — and most misunderstood — exit.

- **Strategic buyers** seek capability, customers, or market position
- **Financial buyers** seek cash flow, scalability, and resale potential

Buyers reward:

- Predictable cash flow
- Clean financials
- Systems and leadership that function without the founder

They discount:

- Founder dependency
- Informal processes
- Hero-based execution

Selling is not storytelling. It is risk reduction.

2. Merging with a Complementary Organization

Mergers combine strength rather than extract value. They work only when:

- Cultures are compatible
- Leadership roles are defined
- Power dynamics are addressed early

A merger is not an exit from responsibility — it is an exit from unilateral control.

3. IPO or Partial Liquidity Events

Rare and demanding. This path requires:

- Strong governance
- Regulatory and reporting readiness
- Leaders comfortable with scrutiny

For most founders, IPOs are not exits — they are transitions into permanent accountability.

4. Licensing Intellectual Property or Operating Systems

An exit that decouples value from operations. It works when:

- IP is clearly defined
- Delivery is standardized
- Brand and enforcement are protected

You cannot license what only exists in your head.

5. Stepping Back While Retaining Ownership

Some founders exit operations, not equity:

- Appointing a CEO
- Moving into a board role
- Reducing day-to-day involvement

This requires the same maturity as a sale: leadership depth, decision clarity, and system reliability. Without that, founders often "return from exit" because they never truly left.

The Hidden Truth About Exit Paths

Each exit option tests a different aspect of maturity:

- Sales expose dependency
- Mergers expose culture
- IPOs expose governance
- Licensing exposes clarity
- Step-backs expose leadership gaps

The right question is not *"How do I exit?"* It is *"What must this organization become to make any exit viable?"*

You do not choose an exit at the end. You **earn it** through how you built leadership, systems, decisions, and accountability beyond yourself.

Next: Chapter 12.2 examines what buyers, successors, and investors actually look for — and how exit readiness is built long before negotiations begin.

12.2. Preparing for Exit — Valuation, Readiness, and Negotiation Power

Most founders think exit preparation begins when a buyer appears. In reality, it begins long before anyone asks.

Valuation is not negotiated into existence. It is *judged*. Two companies with similar revenue can receive radically different offers because buyers price *risk, clarity, and confidence*.

Valuation Is a Proxy for Risk

Buyers do not pay for potential. They pay for predictability. Every weakness increases perceived risk — and risk lowers price, increases earn-outs, or delays payment. What founders often experience as "unfair discounts" are simply signals of uncertainty. Common valuation killers include:

- Founder-dependent decision-making
- Inconsistent or unclear financials
- Informal or undocumented processes
- Customer concentration risk
- Leadership gaps below the top
- Cultural instability during change

These issues do not appear suddenly. They accumulate quietly when exit is postponed as a future concern.

What Buyers and Investors Actually Look For

Across strategic buyers, private equity, and institutional investors, expectations converge around a few signals:

1. Financial Clarity

- Clean, auditable financials
- Predictable cash flow
- Clear unit economics
- Separation of personal and business expenses

2. Operational Independence

- Systems that run without founder intervention
- Documented workflows and decision rights
- Clear accountability

3. Leadership Continuity

- Leaders capable of running the business post-exit
- Succession coverage for key roles
- Evidence of real delegation — not promises

4. Transferable Culture

- Standards that hold under pressure
- Alignment between stated values and behavior
- Low reliance on charisma or personality

Founders often think buyers are evaluating *them*. Buyers are evaluating **how easily the business can live without them.**

Preparation Changes the Power Dynamic

When exit readiness is high:

- Negotiation leverage increases
- Terms improve
- Earn-outs shrink
- Timelines shorten

- Optionality expands

When readiness is low:

- Buyers control the narrative
- Discounts multiply
- Conditions increase
- Pressure rises

I've seen founders with strong businesses accept poor terms because they *needed* the deal. I've also seen smaller companies command premium outcomes because buyers felt confident they could operate them without disruption. *Preparation is leverage.*

Exit Readiness Is Built, Not Declared

Exit readiness is not a six-month checklist. It is the result of years of disciplined design:

- Decisions documented, not improvised
- Leaders empowered, not deferred to the founder
- Systems enforced, not explained
- Culture institutionalized, not admired

Companies designed for exit are also more resilient, investable, stable, and valuable — even if they never sell.

A Quiet but Critical Shift

At this stage, founders must shift identity — from indispensable operator to architect of continuity. The moment a founder becomes replaceable, the organization becomes valuable.

That truth is uncomfortable. It is also unavoidable.

Next: We examine what actually happens *after* exit — patterns from exits that created freedom and those that produced regret, and what founders consistently underestimate when they step away.

12.3. Exit Outcomes — Successes, Failures, and the Truth They Reveal

Exit is an amplifier. It does not create new realities — it exposes existing ones. I've seen founders exit with impressive numbers and deep regret. I've also seen modest exits produce peace, pride, and clarity. The difference is not luck or timing. It is alignment.

What Successful Exits Have in Common

Across industries, successful exits consistently share a few conditions.

1. The Organization Was Not Founder-Centric
The business functioned without daily founder intervention. Leaders made decisions. Systems enforced standards. Customers trusted the organization — not just the founder. Buyers sensed continuity, not fragility.

2. Preparation Began Years Earlier
Founders did not scramble. Financials were clean. Documentation existed. Questions were anticipated. Exit was not a surprise — it was an option kept open. This reduced stress, improved terms, and preserved dignity.

3. The Exit Aligned With Personal Values
Financial outcomes were acceptable — but more importantly, psychologically coherent. Founders knew why they were exiting and what came next. Because identity had expanded beyond the business, exit felt like transition, not loss.

Patterns Behind Difficult or Disappointing Exits

Painful exits emerge from unresolved tensions that surface under pressure.

1. Last-Minute Readiness
Systems rushed. Leaders promoted prematurely. Stories replaced evidence. Buyers noticed — and adjusted terms.

2. Leadership Dependency
When the business required founder presence, buyers discounted heavily or imposed long earn-outs. Some deals collapsed entirely. Profitability existed. Transferability did not.

3. Emotional Unpreparedness
Some founders exited financially but struggled personally. Without clarity around identity or purpose, emptiness and regret followed — even after "successful" deals.

4. Cultural Breakdown During Transition
When teams were excluded or misled, trust eroded. Talent left. Value leaked. Even strong deals deteriorated post-close when culture was mishandled.

Exit Reveals Design Quality

Exit outcomes are not random. They reflect earlier design choices:

- Was leadership built or hoarded?
- Were systems documented or memorized?
- Was culture enforced or assumed?
- Was governance proactive or reactive?
- Did humility survive success?

Founders do not get lucky at exit. They arrive there.

A Quiet Truth Few Founders Hear

A strong exit is not the reward for building a company. It is the reward for **letting go of control at the right pace.** Founders who delay delegation delay exit readiness. Those who equate importance with indispensability make themselves harder to replace — and harder to buy out.

The irony is simple: **the more responsibly a founder steps back, the more valuable the organization becomes.**

What This Means for You

Exit is not a finish line. It is a condition you either build toward — or quietly undermine. The real question is no longer:

- *Can someone buy this business?*

It is:

- *Can this business thrive without me?*

If the answer is yes, exit becomes optional. If the answer is no, exit becomes urgent — and expensive.

Next: In *12.4. Life After Exit*, we examine what happens once the deal is done — and why preparation for life beyond the business often determines whether success expands or collapses after the transaction.

12.4. Life After Exit — Identity, Reinvention, and the Next Chapter

No spreadsheet prepares you for this part. After the exit, life changes quickly — and not always predictably. Depending on the deal, you may step away immediately, remain through a transition, or stay on in a defined role. Often, <u>non-compete or non-solicitation clauses limit your ability to do the work that once defined you.</u>

If you step away fully, the shift can be abrupt. Meetings stop. Urgency fades. The calendar opens. Titles disappear. For the first time in years — sometimes decades — there is space. And space is revealing.

Some founders thrive immediately. Others feel disoriented. Many experience a quiet grief they didn't anticipate — not because the exit was wrong, but because the business had become a primary source of identity, structure, and meaning.

This is why exit should never be treated as an endpoint. *It is a transition* — and transitions demand intention and proactiveness.

Why Life After Exit Is Often Harder Than the Exit Itself

Most founders prepare extensively for valuation, negotiation, and deal mechanics. Far fewer prepare for what happens after the close, after the wire transfer clears. Common post-exit challenges include:

- Loss of identity, purpose, meaning, or relevance
- Sudden absence of authority and decision-making
- Disrupted routines and purpose
- Relationship strain due to shifting expectations
- Pressure to "do something big" too quickly

None of these signal failure. They signal that the founder optimized for *transaction* — not *transition*.

Founders Who Thrive After Exit Share Key Traits

1. Identity Was Not Exclusively Tied to the Company
The business was something they led — not who they were. They already saw themselves as builders, mentors, investors, learners, or contributors beyond a single role.

2. They Allowed a Season of Decompression
They paused. Reflected. Reconnected with neglected parts of life. This was not stagnation — it was integration.

3. They Redefined Contribution, Not Just Income
Some invested. Some advised. Some taught or served. Some chose quieter forms of impact. The question shifted from *What do I build next?* to *How do I want to contribute now?*

The Risk of Rushing Reinvention

One of the most common post-exit mistakes is immediately chasing the next high. Founders jump into new ventures without clarity. They accept roles they don't enjoy. They mistake activity for healing. *Reinvention without reflection often recreates the same patterns that led to burnout or constraint before the exit.* Wise founders slow down — not because they lack drive, but because they respect the transition.

Roles, Non-Competes, and Psychological Closure

Many exits include temporary roles — advisor, executive, ambassador. These can work when boundaries are clear. Problems arise when:

- Roles are vague
- Authority is ambiguous
- Terms are not clear
- Emotional attachment remains unresolved

Closure is not abandonment. It is completion. <u>Founders who exit well allow the organization to evolve without them — and allow themselves to evolve beyond it.</u>

Legacy Is What Continues Without You

The deepest satisfaction after exit rarely comes from the number. It comes from endurance:

- Leaders you developed succeeding
- Culture holding under new ownership
- Systems functioning without intervention
- Independence replacing dependence

Exit is not about cashing out. It is about closing one chapter with integrity so the next can begin with freedom.

1. Some founders build again.
2. Some invest.
3. Some teach, mentor, or serve.
4. Some rest — and that is not failure.

The goal was never just to build something that grows. It was to build something that:

- Lasts
- Transfers
- Creates value beyond you
- And gives you the freedom to choose what comes next

That is what a great exit makes possible.

Reflect & Practice

Reflection Prompts

- What part of your identity would feel most disrupted if you stepped away tomorrow?
- Which elements of the business still depend on your personal judgment, relationships, or presence?

- What kind of life do you want *after* ownership changes — and is the business being designed to support that?

Practice Challenge (14 Days)

Over the next weeks:

1. Write a one-page **Exit Intent Statement** defining purpose, flexibility, and non-negotiables (not valuation).
2. Identify **one dependency** that would block a clean exit — and begin removing it.
3. Create or update a document titled **"If I Were Gone Tomorrow"** outlining what must still function without you.

Exit clarity does not accelerate departure.
It strengthens design, discipline, and optionality — long before exit becomes necessary.

Exit clarity does not accelerate departure. It strengthens design, discipline, and optionality — long before exit becomes necessary.

Putting It All Together

CONCLUSION
Putting It All Together

This isn't the end of your journey. It's the moment you stop building blindly — and start building deliberately, with scale, exit, and legacy in mind.

You've just walked a path most founders never fully complete. Not because they lack desire, intelligence, or effort — but because they were never given a complete roadmap. You now have one.

This book was not written to hype entrepreneurship. It was written to discipline it. You didn't just learn how to start something. You learned how to *design, build, stabilize, scale, and exit something that lasts*. That distinction changes everything.

This book was not written to hype entrepreneurship. It was written to *discipline it*. You didn't just learn how to start something. You learned how to design and scale it to last. And that distinction changes everything.

What You've Built — The Framework at a Glance

Part I: Purpose & Design

You clarified what most founders rush past:

- The problem worth solving
- The purpose behind the work

- The identity, positioning, business model, structure, and strategic logic required to support scale and exit

You learned that scale is not something you add later. It is something you *design for early.*

Part II: Form & Legalize

You translated intention into reality:

- Foundational documents and strategic plans
- Legal, financial, and operational infrastructure
- Teams, advisors, and early culture

You moved from idea to institution — without skipping the disciplines that protect long-term value.

Part III: Launch & Stabilize

You learned how to:

- Test before you announce
- Deliver before you accelerate
- Stabilize before you scale
- Replace audacity with systems

You discovered that momentum without structure creates fragility — not freedom.

Part IV: Scale & Exit

You explored:

- Multiple scaling vehicles and tradeoffs
- The principles and disciplines that sustain growth
- Leadership behaviors that prevent scale from breaking
- Exit strategy, preparation, execution, and life beyond the deal

You learned that scale does not reward effort.
It rewards **clarity, discipline, and coherence**.

What Changed Along the Way

1. You now design more deliberately
2. You form with greater intentionality
3. You launch with less noise and more signal
4. You stabilize before expanding
5. You scale without losing control
6. You prepare for exit without fear or regret

This is not theory. <u>It is a framework. It is a roadmap.</u> It is an operating system for founders.

Integration Is Where the Real Work Begins

Reading builds awareness. Application builds mastery.

Lasting organizations are not built in bursts of motivation — but through rhythm, reflection, and disciplined repetition.

From this point forward:

- Think in systems, not moments
- Think in cycles, not sprints
- Think in design decisions, not reactions

Your 30–60–90 Day Founder Reset

No matter where you are on the *Scale to Last* journey — forming, launching, scaling, or preparing to exit — this reset helps you re-anchor with intention.

Days 1–30: Reground the Foundation

- Revisit your problem, purpose, and positioning
- Identify one design flaw quietly limiting growth
- Clarify your scaling and exit intent
- Strengthen one core system (finance, operations, leadership, or delivery)

Days 31–60: Strengthen Structure

- Reduce founder dependency in one critical area
- Document one high-impact process
- Improve financial visibility and predictability
- Elevate one key leader or advisor relationship

Days 61–90: Prepare for the Next Phase

- Conduct a scale-readiness or exit-readiness self-assessment
- Eliminate one bottleneck slowing momentum
- Remove one barrier undermining scale
- Align leadership, culture, and systems with where you are going — not where you started
- Set the next 90-day design or redesign priorities

Organizations drift when founders stop designing and redesigning. You now know how not to.

Founder "Preflight" Checklist

Before growth, capital, or exit conversations, ask:

1. Is our problem definition still accurate?
2. Is our purpose still guiding decisions?
3. Does our identity still hold as we grow?
4. Is the business model profitable and scalable?
5. Does structure support capital, talent, and exit?
6. Can the organization function without me?
7. Are systems replacing prowess?
8. Is the culture strong enough to carry scale?

9. Do leaders know what "great" looks like?
10. Are we building value — or just activity?

If you can answer these clearly, you are not guessing. You are building with intention.

Final Note

The ultimate goal was never just to build something that grows. It was to build something that *lasts* — gives you *freedom of choice*, and leaves behind a <u>legacy stronger than your presence</u>.

You now have the discipline to do exactly that.

Next Steps

NEXT STEPS

Finishing this book gives you clarity. What you do next builds capability. *Scale to Last* was designed as a complete framework — but frameworks create impact only when they are practiced, reinforced, and applied in real operating environments. To support founders beyond the page, *The A to Z Institute* offers several ways to deepen implementation.

1. One-on-One Founder & Executive Coaching

For founders navigating critical transitions and high-stakes decisions, including:

- Scaling without losing control
- Leadership expansion and succession readiness
- Capital, partnership, or exit preparation
- Complex strategic or organizational inflection points

Personalized. Confidential. Outcome-driven.

Learn more about how our coaching works at www.TheAtoZInstitute.com

2. Team Workshops & Organizational Programs

Designed for leadership teams preparing for scale or exit. Programs include:

- Scale and exit readiness workshops
- Systems, execution, and accountability design
- Culture and leadership alignment at scale
- Founder transition and successor preparation

✉ To schedule a discovery conversation, contact
info@TheAtoZInstitute.com

3. Founder Mastermind (Group Coaching)

A facilitated peer environment for founders building intentionally.
Includes:

- Live coaching and strategic reviews
- Peer accountability and shared learning
- Design, scale, and exit decision support
- Tools, frameworks, and guided implementation

Apply or join the waitlist to participate.

4. Scale to Last Venture Lab

A selective, operator-led partnership for founders ready to scale with
discipline and exit optionality. The Venture Lab provides:

- Embedded strategic and operating support
- Leadership depth and decision architecture
- Reduced founder dependency and execution risk
- Scale and exit readiness built into operations

Hands-on. Limited capacity. Selective by design.

5. Scale to Last Masterclass

A practical, video-based experience helping founders apply the
framework with clarity. This masterclass covers:

• Designing for scale and exit from day one
• Stabilizing before expansion
• Choosing the right scaling vehicles
• Building leadership depth

Self-paced. Launching soon.

7. Scale to Last Online Course

For founders ready to operationalize the full framework across their organization. This course includes:

• Structured lessons across each phase
• Scale and exit readiness roadmaps
• Systems, delegation, and financial tools
• Leadership and succession guides

Coming soon.

Finally, you don't need more information. You need the *right* structure, discipline, and support to apply what you already know.

Whatever path you choose next, build with intention. That is how organizations scale — and how founders last.

ADDITIONAL RESOURCES

Grow Across All Dimensions of Leadership and Influence

As a professional, leader, investor, or entrepreneur—thinking strategically is essential. But lasting success requires depth across multiple dimensions of leadership, communication, influence, and personal mastery.

To truly stand out, scale your impact, and thrive in complex environments, you must master the inner game, the relationship game, the communication game, and the execution game.

That's why **The A to Z Institute** offers a full suite of current and upcoming programs designed to support your growth far beyond this book. Each program is (or will be) available in multiple formats—webinars, workshops, coaching, online courses, and books—so you can learn in the way that best fits your goals and your schedule.

These complementary competencies help you (and your team) grow into a more complete communicator, leader, and influencer:

1. Speaking for Impact: Communicate with Confidence, Clarity, and Credibility.

Develop the speaking skills that elevate your leadership. Learn how to craft messages that connect, deliver with presence, engage audiences, and speak with authority in meetings, pitches, and presentations.

2. Strategic Edge: Think Clearly, Plan Smart, and Execute with Impact

Cut through complexity, sharpen your judgment, and turn vision into focused action. This program helps leaders and entrepreneurs build critical thinking, strategic clarity, and execution discipline to drive meaningful results and long-term advantage.

3. 360 Communication: Speak with Clarity. Connect with Impact.

Master communication across every medium—verbal, nonverbal, written, and visual. Learn to articulate ideas clearly, lead teams effectively, and communicate with confidence in all settings.

4. Conflict & Negotiation: Turn Tension into Transformation.

Stop avoiding difficult conversations. Learn how to navigate disagreements, negotiate win–win outcomes, and transform conflict into collaboration and stronger relationships.

5. Emotional Fitness: Build the Inner Strength to Win the Outer 5ame.

You can't lead others if you aren't leading yourself. Strengthen your resilience, emotional regulation, and inner stability so you can perform at your best under pressure.

6. Feedback Exchanges: Give and Receive Feedback Like a Pro.

Transform feedback into a catalyst for growth. Learn to deliver feedback with clarity and care—and receive it with openness—so you build trust, alignment, and continuous improvement.

7. Creating & Transforming Culture: Shape the Soul of Your Organization.

Culture determines performance. Learn frameworks for assessing, shaping, and sustaining a culture where people thrive and values become lived behaviors.

8. Leadership Transitions: Succeed at Every Level.

Every leadership stage requires new skills. From first-time supervisor to executive leader, this program prepares you to lead with confidence at any level.

9. Presence to Authority: Lead with Influence and Build Credibility That Scales

Command the room, communicate with confidence, and position yourself as a trusted authority. This program helps leaders and professionals elevate presence, expand influence, and turn credibility into lasting impact and results.

10. The Psychology & Habits of High Performers: Unlock Your Inner Greatness.

Greatness is intentional. Discover the mental models, rituals, and performance habits used by elite performers—and learn how to apply them to your own leadership and life.

11. Rewiring Your Brain: Upgrade Your Thinking. Recode Your Future.

Break free from old patterns. Apply neuroscience-backed strategies to reshape your beliefs, rewire your mindset, and accelerate personal and professional growth.

12. Your Complete Marketing Engine: Attract, Nurture, Convert — on Repeat

Build a credible digital presence. Capture the right leads. Automate follow-up and conversion. Create a repeatable marketing system that supports scale without constant manual effort or tech overwhelm.

To explore these and other founder-focused programs, visit **The A to Z Institute** website.

You'll find masterclasses, online courses, and upcoming books that build on the frameworks in this one — supporting you through design, formation, launch, stabilization, scale, and exit.

P.S. If you lead a leadership team, portfolio company, or growing organization, consider bringing one or more of these programs as a webinar, workshop, or cohort experience. Founder clarity sets direction — but aligned teams are what turn strategy into lasting enterprise value.

Additional Resources

CONNECT WITH US

You're now part of a community of founders and builders committed to designing organizations that last — beyond hustle, beyond hype, and beyond dependency on any one person.

Stay connected and continue the journey through:

- **The A to Z Institute website and insights**
- **LinkedIn** (long-form thinking, frameworks, and founder conversations)
- **YouTube** (educational videos, interviews, & strategic breakdowns)
- **Our email community** (tools, templates, and early access)

You'll receive practical resources, invitations to private sessions, summits, and workshops, and first access to new books and programs that expand on the *Scale to Last* framework.

If this book helped you think more clearly, design more intentionally, or approach scale and exit with greater confidence, I'd truly appreciate a short *review* on **Amazon**. Your perspective helps other founders find a more disciplined, sustainable path forward.

FINAL WORD

You don't need to rush.
You don't need to chase scale.
You don't need to force an exit.

You need clarity.
You need discipline.
You need design.

Scale to Last was written to give you something most founders never receive: a complete roadmap — not just to start, but to build, stabilize, scale, and eventually step away without regret.

You now understand that growth without structure creates fragility. That scale without discipline creates dependence. And that exit without preparation creates loss — of value, of legacy, or of self.

Whether you choose to scale aggressively, grow steadily, step back, or eventually exit, you now have the frameworks to do so intentionally — on your terms.

Your future as a founder will not happen by accident.
You will design it.

Build wisely.
Stabilize before you scale.
Scale with intention.
Exit when — and if — it serves your life and purpose.

And leave behind something strong enough to outlast you.

www.ingramcontent.com/pod-product-compliance
Lightning Source LLC
LaVergne TN
LVHW052025080426
835513LV00018B/2158